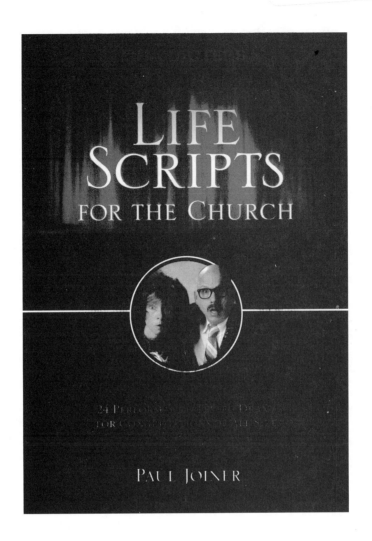

LIFE SCRIPTS

FOR THE CHURCH

24 Performance-Tested Dramas
For Congregations of All Sizes

PAUL JOINER

NELSON REFERENCE & ELECTRONIC
A Division of Thomas Nelson Publishers
Since 1798

www.thomasnelson.com

LIFE SCRIPTS

FOR THE CHURCH

Volume 1

Volume II

Characters

Holiday

More than 400 individual scripts available online
for purchase and download

www.thomasnelson.com/drama

LIFE SCRIPTS
FOR THE CHURCH

24 PERFORMANCE-TESTED DRAMAS
FOR CONGREGATIONS OF ALL SIZES!

PAUL JOINER

Published in Nashville, Tennessee, by Thomas Nelson, Inc.

Nelson books may be purchased in bulk for educational, business,
fundraising, or sales promotion use. For information, please email
SpecialMarkets@ThomasNelson.com.

Nelson books may also be purchased in bulk for ministry use by churches,
parachurch ministries, and media ministries. For information, please call
(800) 251-4000 ext. 2804 or email NelsonMinistryServices@thomasnelson.com.

All Scripture quotations, unless otherwise noted, are taken from the
King James Version of the Bible.

Managing Editor W. Mark Whitlock
Edited by Steffany Woolsey
Book packaging by Design Point, Inc.
Interior Design by Bennett Davis Group

Library of Congress Cataloging-in-Publication Data available upon request.

Printed in the United States of America

ISBN: 1418509876

06 07 08 09 10 11 12 RRD 9 8 7 6 5 4 3 2 1

A Word
About Copyrights

Wait a minute. Wait! Stop the show. Hold the curtain. Don't cue the lights.
Hold everything.

The side-splitting and soul-touching scripts you hold in your hand were
written for you. Paul Joiner and Thomas Nelson can't wait to see
God use you and drama in your local church.

We want you to win.

We've built the copyright rules to help you put on these productions
with the least amount of struggle.

DO make copies of the scripts for your actors, technical crew,
and pastoral staff.

DON'T keep them. After the production is complete, please destroy them.

DO tell your peers about the success you're having with drama.

DON'T lend those copies or your book to other churches. If they want
to see samples, please send them to www.thomasnelson.com/drama
for more information.

DO include the dramas on any recordings you make of your services.

DON'T sell copies of the performances only. It's fine to include the presentation
of a script in the context of your worship service. However, when you
sell copies of your presentation of a script by itself or with other dramas,
you're breaking the copyright. You'll need to secure permission from us
before you do so. Send your request on church letterhead to:
Nelson Reference, P.O. Box 141000, Nashville, TN 37214.

DON'T forget to put credits on the recordings. Here's a sample sentence
for you. "The dramatic presentation, 'Heavenly Hash,' is used by permission
of the author and Thomas Nelson, Inc. ©2006 Paul Joiner."

DO tell us about how God is using the dramas in your life.
Go to www.thomasnelson.com, click on "contact us," and send us an email.

May God richly bless you . . . and your audiences.
May your productions point to the Cross.

Sincerely,

The Publisher

Characters

Table of Contents

Introduction

You are about to meet some of the most interesting people you will ever find in the plotline of a drama sketch. Characters, every one!

Gus and Gladys Glum live a miserable existence, yet you can't help loving them to pieces. They'll rain on your parade, wear the same clothes every time they make an appearance, and refuse to get along with anyone (including each other). Gus and Gladys are the couple you love to hate. But you better watch it—because you'll find a special place in your heart for these two.

Dan and Jan got lost somewhere in the eighties. Their wardrobes, hairstyles, and mannerisms are just as mystifying as their theology. These two are deeply in love and not ashamed to make googly eyes over each other as they desperately try to explain biblical themes they know nothing about.

Then there are **Bridget and Brandon**, the over-the-top talk show hosts who can invoke something sensational from the simplest subject. You'll have a difficult time deciding what they're more excited about—the guests on their show or their own close-ups! Nonetheless, a strong message always accompanies their madness.

You never know what's going to happen when **Rachel and Roger** show up. These two are larger than life. But despite their best intentions, everything they touch turns into a disaster.

Finally you'll meet a homeless couple, **Cecil and Penelope,** who live in the city park. Though they are slightly mentally disabled, their childlike faith is infectious. No one who encounters these sweet, giving characters leaves unchanged. Cecil and Penelope are an endearing presence on any platform.

....

A few nights ago I had this dream . . . and it was a bit scary. I dreamed I was being confronted by Gus & Gladys, Jan & Dan, and Cecil & Penelope. The dream went something like this:

SCENE	DREAM SEQUENCE
	(PAUL is in his bedroom and awakens to find that his worst nightmare has come true! GUS and GLADYS, JAN and DAN, and CECIL and PENELOPE are standing around the bed staring over him.)
Paul:	Aaagh! What is going on? What are you all doing in my room? Don't you know it's 3 A.M.?
Gus:	We've got a bone to pick with you, bucko!
Gladys:	That's right! And we're ready to rumble!
Paul:	With me? Why?
Jan:	Well, it appears we're all having image problems!
Paul:	Image problems! You're not even real people . . .
Dan:	But that's not what church congregations think!
Cecil:	People think Penelope and I are real.
Penelope:	They laugh and cry every time we show up.
Paul:	I know, but . . .
Gus:	Let's cut to the chase, pal! We're having a little difficulty accepting ourselves for who you created us to be.

Gladys:	You tell 'im, honey!
Paul:	What do you mean?
Dan:	You've created Jan and I to be a little . . . clueless.
Jan:	Especially about Bible matters and such.
Dan:	Like we don't know the Bible starts with the book of Genocide and ends with the book of Revolution!
Jan:	*(Lovingly takes DAN's hand)* Oh no, honey, that's wrong. It's the book of Genesis and the book of Revelation.
Dan:	What did I say?
Jan:	*(Pats DAN's cheek)* You said Genocide and Revolution. But it was cute honey, cute! I just fell in love with you all over again!
Dan:	Jan, it's not our fault we get things so mixed up! Paul created our characters to be this way.
Paul:	Your characters help the congregation understand why it is so important to know their Bible! The more you mix up Scripture, the more the people in the pew feel convicted to spend time in the Word.
Jan:	So you think our big hair, retro outfits, and Bible ignorance drive that point home?
Paul:	I do.
Gladys:	So what about us? You've had me in the same outfit for ten years!
Gus:	Yeah, look at her! No makeup . . . bad hair . . . and glares that could sink a thousand ships!
Gladys:	*(Glares at GUS)* You better watch it!
Gus:	*(Glares back at GLADYS) You* watch it!
Gladys:	*(Back to PAUL)* See what you've done? We're opinionated, grouchy, cantankerous, and . . .
Gus:	People laugh at us!
Gladys:	Yeah, what did you go and do a thing like that for?
Paul:	People aren't laughing *at* you, they're laughing *with* you! You two represent people we all know!
Gus:	So?
Paul:	Each of us relates to you in some way. You're so over-the-top it makes us feel better about ourselves. You break the ice before the pastor comes up to address more sensitive issues like stewardship, relationships, and other tough topics.
Gladys:	So we're icebreakers, huh?
Paul:	That's your purpose!

Penelope:	Then Mr. Paul, what's the purpose of Cecil and me?
Cecil:	Yeah. We don't have a home . . . we live in the park . . . we don't have much to offer.
Penelope:	We aren't very smart either, Mr. Paul. Some people think we have the minds of five-year-olds.
Paul:	And that is why you are so beautiful! You are childlike. The simplicity of your words and the purity of your hearts cause us to laugh, then cry. You make us emotionally vulnerable so we can be moved by the Holy Spirit.
Penelope:	We do that?
Paul:	Yes, you do.
Cecil:	Is that why we will always be a little slow and a lot homeless?
Paul:	Yes. I'm sorry.
Penelope:	Don't be sorry. I love it in the park, and there is no one I'd rather be with than Cecil. He is the smartest and most handsomest man I know.
Paul:	Look . . . all of you. Characters are created to help the audience relate to the message being taught. I can talk about a subject or illustrate that subject through colorful characters like you. People never forget you.
Cecil:	They don't?
Paul:	No. Never.
Jan:	*(Starts reapplying her lipstick)* So you're saying we're unforgettable?
Paul:	Yes!
Gladys:	Hear that, Gus? I'm unforgettable!
Gus:	He's talking about your character, not your bad hair!
Gladys:	*(Picks up a pillow)* You better watch it!
Gus:	*(Picks up another pillow) You* watch it!
	(DAN and JAN, along with CECIL and PENELOPE, break up the pillow fight that ensues between GUS and GLADYS while PAUL crawls back down under the covers.)
SCENE	**FADE TO BLACK**
	END

Characters are unforgettable! (Even in your sleep.) Use them to create a deeper impact in your dramas.

I have noticed that a lot of Christian dramas lack character. What I mean is that the characters in most scripts are one-dimensional, simple, and forgettable. This is why I try to place interesting and unforgettable characters in as many sketches as I can.

When directing sketches that are character driven, there are several important things to keep in mind. The following is a mini course on things to remember when directing or writing character roles.

UNFORGETTABLE CHARACTERS 101

1. Characters are real people.

Unforgettable characters are those that we all somehow know, even if we can't put a finger on it. They represent people in our family, church, workplace, or neighborhood. Unforgettable characters connect the audience to real-life situations. Their behavior speaks of who they are, where they've come from, and what they want. Remember, the audience can spot a fake a mile away.

2. Subtle is more effective than sensational.

Whether in a comedic or dramatic role, actors often go so overboard with their characterization that all the audience sees is an actor playing a character. A good actor transforms himself into a believable character that is accepted as true to life.

3. Be the character first; dress the character second.

First decide the who, what, when, and where of your character. Once you have a good understanding of what makes your character tick, then select the appropriate costume and accessories to support your character's background.

4. Enunciation is more important than accent.

The audience may love a character's actions, but if they can't understand what's being said, you'll bomb. Verbal delivery should support the script and never hinder the message.

5. The foundation for a comedic character is the script, not slapstick.

It's tempting for a comedic actor to go for the gag, gimmick, or shtick. This may be an easy way to get a laugh, but the humor is usually short-lived. A more seasoned actor understands that his character's relation to the plot, even delivery of lines, and reaction to the circumstances being played out onstage are what make good comedy.

6. A character is 80 percent emotional and 20 percent physical.

What is it that makes truly unforgettable characters? Simple: their background, environment, family, experiences, education, socioeconomic standing, and physical characteristics—in short, all the things that make them who they are. Not a pair of oversized sunglasses, a cane, a large foam cowboy hat, or a bad wig. Concentrate first on the emotional makeup of your character; the mannerisms will emerge on their own.

7. Unless the script says so, your actions should not speak louder than your words.

Though you want some of your characters to appear larger than life, there is a limit to how far you can take them physically before their actions will obstruct the dialogue. Find a graceful way to marry your actions with the lines.

8. Don't unload your character at the beginning of the sketch; unveil him throughout.

The more you are around a person, the more you get to know him, right? This also holds true with the characters in a sketch. If you reveal everything about your character in the first few lines of the script, there is nowhere else for you to take him. Slowly divulge the physical and emotional information about your character throughout the course of the drama.

10. Stay away from "custom character kits" when preparing for your role.

Old people don't necessarily wear glasses and use canes. Blondes don't always chew gum when they talk. Tough guys don't always wear leather jackets. Get my drift? Create an unpredictable character. Brand a character like you would a product, making her a distinct and unforgettable individual. Put a little thought into how this old lady, blonde, or tough guy could be different—while remaining believable—from the ones your audience has seen before.

Do you want to help the actors on your drama team learn how to really develop a character? Have them complete this Knowing Your Character exercise.

....

KNOWING YOUR CHARACTER

Before you begin memorizing lines, learning your blocking, or even rehearsing, attaining an accurate grasp of your character is vital.

Your first glimpse into the mind and mannerisms of your character can be found in the content of the script. What it does *and* doesn't tell you are both crucial pieces of information. Delivery, timing, emotional motivation, and reasoning all stem from figuring out who your character truly is.

A. What the script tells you.

As you read through the script, ask yourself the following questions:

1. Does the script outright reveal any of the following information about my character?

 a. age
 b. temperament
 c. health/disabilities
 d. family life/marital status
 e. idiosyncrasies
 f. environmental influences
 g. occupation
 h. childhood surroundings
 i. background
 j. clothing
 k. hairstyle

2. What is my character's connection to the plotline?

a. antagonist or protagonist
b. leading role or secondary role
c. positive or negative
d. substantiating or supporting

3. What is my character's correlation to the drama's underlying message?

a. What purpose and meaning are behind the creation of my character?
b. Who in the audience will identify with my role?
c. What secondary element of my character's role might I focus on instead of focusing on the purpose of my role?

4. Are there any recurring phrases, words, patterns, or habits my character exhibits?

B. What the script doesn't tell you.

Ask yourself the following questions when deciding how to portray your character. Sometimes making up a "history" of a person helps you create a deeper understanding of that character. This is an exercise in imagination and make-believe!

1. Who was your character before the script?

a. How did he arrive where he is now?
b. What are his family and geographic backgrounds?
c. What has caused him to have the attitudes and feelings that he exhibits in the piece?

2. What is going on inside?

a. What motivates her? What discourages her?
b. What kinds of books would she read? Why?
c. What political affiliation would she have?
d. Where would she hang out in her free time?
e. What are her hobbies?
f. What makes her laugh?
g. What makes her cry? *Would* she cry?
h. What kinds of people make up her close circle of friends?
i. Is there anything in her past that might drastically affect what she does today?

3. How does your director want you to play your character?

a. Has the director given you instruction on how to play the role?
b. How much freedom do you have in creating your character?

Now that you better understand what makes a character tick, get to know Gus and Gladys, Jan and Dan, Bridget and Brandon, Rachel and Roger, and the beautifully insightful Cecil and Penelope. Then adapt these scripts to your talent, facility, and service.

Go on, now—get out there and create unforgettable characters.

Lights! Camera! Ministry!

HIS understudy,

Paul Joiner

Welcome to the Wonderful & Wacky World of
JAN & DAN

The following five dramas feature the wild and wacky world of Jan & Dan. Stuck somewhere in a time warp, Jan & Dan are a reality blast from the past. This married couple is polite, kind, friendly, and will invite you over at the drop of a hat for Jell-O and a friendly game of Twister.

Ask them any Bible question and they'll give you an answer. Now, it probably isn't the *right* answer . . . but you have to give them credit for coming up with something pretty close to the real thing.

Still madly in love with each other, Jan & Dan view the world through rose-colored lenses. Their infectious humor is sure to be a hit in your church. Don't be surprised if they receive a warm reception every Sunday they make an appearance.

Here are a few Drama Cues to help you produce the sketches featuring Jan & Dan.

Image

Jan & Dan are a little bit behind the times. Their syrupy sweet nature places them somewhere in the 1960s or '70s. Pristine, perfect, self-righteous, together, and well-planned!

Wardrobe

Dress Jan & Dan in retro clothes always matching in color and style. I like to envision Jan's hairstyle as a big bouffant hairdo, with Dan's hair almost as big. Though all of their friends live in the here and now, Dan & Jan seem to be oblivious that they are stuck in the past.

Love Birds

Even after many years of marriage, this couple is still very much in love. They are kind and polite to one another . . . almost ad nauseam. They love to sit close, hold hands, and wink and smile at each other like they're on a first date. This kind of interaction adds hilarity to the utopian world they inhabit.

Set

Most of the Jan & Dan sketches take place in their home. Try to give the set a retro feel with furniture and household accessories that look like they're from the sixties. You don't want a hippie/bohemian look; rather, a set more like what you'd see in a middle-class conservative home: neat, orderly, and with everything in its place.

Paul's Favorites

I absolutely love Jan & Dan. The following are my two favorite Jan & Dan sketches and the *Life Scripts* volumes they can be found in:

Bible Balderdash / *Life Scripts: Volume I*
Heavenly Hash / *Life Scripts: Characters*

Want some ideas about what Jan & Dan might look like? Check out photos of the original clueless love birds at www.pauljoiner.com and meet Jan & Dan.

And now, Jan and Dan!

HEAVENLY HASH

with Jan and Dan

TOPIC

Heaven: What is heaven really like?

SYNOPSIS

After-dinner conversation turns to a discussion on heaven,
but when a couple of new Christians turn to Dan and Jan for answers,
the truth of heaven is turned upside down.

SETS/PROPS

Sketch takes place in the living room of Jan and Dan's home. Couch,
chairs, and a coffee table are required. Each character has a glass of soda
in his or her hand.

CHARACTERS

Dan – Christian; husband to Jan

Jan – Christian; wife to Dan

Larry – New Christian, husband to Terry

Terry – New Christian; wife to Larry

LIGHTS:	**BLACKOUT** *(Actors move into place)*
SOUND:	**MUSICAL TRANSITION INTO SKETCH**
GRAPHIC:	**TITLE SLIDE—** *Heavenly Hash* with Jan & Dan
LIGHTS:	**UP ON STAGE**

(DAN and JAN are entertaining LARRY and TERRY in the living room of their home. They have finished dinner and are relaxing together . . . JAN holds a plate of brownies.)

Jan: Would any of you care for an after-dinner brownie?

Larry: Oh, no thank you.

Terry: I don't think we could eat another thing!

Dan: Aren't they fat free, Jan?

Jan: They certainly are.

Dan: They're fat free! Eat without guilt!

Larry: Really . . . no thank you.

Jan: Okay, then. Would you like to gather around the piano and sing American folk songs, or shall we get the karaoke machine out?

Dan: You should hear Jan belt out *Puff the Magic Dragon*! Or, *If I Had A Hammer!*

Terry: Actually, Larry and I had a few questions we'd like to ask you.

Dan: Questions?

(Everyone sits down.)

Larry: As you know, Terry and I recently moved here from the Midwest. As new Christians attending First Church here in town, we've discovered that there are a lot of things about the Bible we don't understand yet.

Dan: I'm sorry.

Terry: And we're just a little confused about something.

Jan: I thought you looked confused ever since you moved to California.

Dan: So what is it that you're confused about?

Terry & Larry: Heaven.

Jan & Dan: Heaven?

Larry: Yeah, we've got some questions about heaven. And we thought that since you two have been Christians for years, maybe you could help us.

▸ *Drama Cue: Dialogue First*

Cleverly crafted dialogue can carry a great comedy sketch, even without any physical humor. In a sketch like this one, the main focus during both rehearsals and performances should be on good, clean delivery of lines. Characterization should always take a backseat to the words being spoken.

▸ *Characterization: Jan & Dan Moment*

It is very important to Jan & Dan that they are doing everything "right." Be sure their hair, clothes, refreshments, and home are perfectly in order.

Terry:	For instance, we've heard heaven called by other names . . . does heaven have other names?
Dan:	Heaven . . . heaven . . . Uh, Jan, why don't you take this one.
Jan:	Uh . . . I'm drawing a blank . . . drawing a blank . . . Dan, why don't you go ahead, precious?
Dan:	Heaven. Heaven is also called paradise! The celestial city! The city of angels . . .
Jan:	. . . the City of Lights . . .
Dan:	. . . the city that never sleeps . . .
Jan:	. . . the City of Brotherly Love . . .
Dan:	. . . and we mustn't forget, the Emerald City! Beautiful green . . .
Jan:	Honey, no. Not the Emerald City. The Emerald City is that place in *The Wizard of Oz.*
Dan:	Oh, that's right. The reason I said that is because of the yellow brick road that runs through heaven.
Jan:	That's right! You're so smart, dear!
Terry:	Wait, I thought it was streets of gold, not the yellow brick road.
Dan:	Yellow, gold, maize, mustard . . . they're all in the same color palette.
Jan:	Yeah, the important thing is that we will be there, isn't it?
Larry:	What will heaven look like?
Jan:	Okay, well, from what we've heard, it's very lovely. It's not like anyone went there for a weekend and came back with pictures.
Dan:	We just have to take His Word for it that it's a really swanky place.
Terry:	What will we do in heaven?
Dan:	Jan . . .
Jan:	Dan, I think you should take this one . . . .
Dan:	Well, we know that we will be . . . playing harps . . .
Jan:	Cloud racing . . .
Dan:	Walking around in awe with our mouths open . . .
Jan:	Possibly getting autographs from some of the "biggies" up there!
Dan:	Floating will be a part of our day.
Jan:	And, oh, we'll be setting up house!
Larry:	Setting up house?

▸ *Characterization: Jan & Dan Moment*

Jan & Dan should always sit side by side so they can react to and play off each other.

▸ *Caution: Pause for Crowd Reactions*
When a comedy "works," actors will hear laughter from the audience. They need to pause in order to let the audience react, then continue only when the laughter begins to subside. Stay in the moment, keep your focus, don't break character, and when the time is right . . . continue. You don't want your audience to miss any dialogue.

Jan:	That's right! You know, we're all getting mansions up there! So we'll have to pick out the carpet, the drapes, tile . . . you know . . . that will take some time.
Larry:	I thought the Bible said that Jesus was preparing us a place.
Jan & Dan:	Okay . . .
Dan:	But we can at least pitch in when we get there and help out. . . . I mean, He built the house.
Larry:	And will we eat up there?
Jan:	Well, of course, silly. We'll dine on . . . angel food cake . . .
Dan:	Milk and honey will be all over the place . . . you'll have to be careful where you step!
Jan:	And lamb, apparently a big supper with lamb!
Terry:	Is that before or after we get our new bodies?
Dan:	New bodies?
Terry:	I thought the Bible said that we would have new, perfect bodies?
Dan:	Well, sort of. Actually we just get one of three choices: A heart, a brain, or some courage.
Jan:	Oh, no, honey.
Dan:	What? What did I say?
Jan:	You said a heart, a brain, or courage. That, too, was from *The Wizard of Oz*!
Dan:	Oh, what I meant to say is that we'll all get a clean, pure brain and heart when we get to our heavenly home.
Jan:	That's right, because *there's no place like home! There's no place like home!*
Larry:	And there will be no more crying!
Dan:	No more crying, sighing, or lying.
Jan:	No aging! I can't wait to take advantage of that one!
Dan:	We'll all be wearing white!
Jan:	Have hair, just like me!
Dan:	And conversations like this can go on for eternity, because there isn't any time there.
Jan:	So the four of us can sit and chat for the likes of thousands of years on end.
	(LARRY and TERRY look at each other in shock.)
Terry:	*(Standing)* I think we should go.

▸ *Characterization: Jan & Dan Moment*

When Dan or Jan makes a verbal mistake, they giggle and gloss right over it. They are not trying to cover their errors; they are simply clueless and think that their second wrong answer is the right one!

Larry:	*(Standing)* Yes, we've got to go.
Dan:	*(Standing)* Why, are you in a hurry? I was just about to tell you about the little people that live outside the gates of heaven . . . They sing . . . there is a mayor . . .
Jan:	*(Standing)* And you haven't even taken a bite out of my brownies . . . it's a heavenly hash recipe.
Terry:	Thank you, but we have to rescue our babysitter.
Dan:	We'll just pick up where we left off another night.
Larry:	We appreciate the information about heaven.
Terry:	Yeah, but I must say, the details sound very different from what I heard growing up.
Jan:	Well, honey, you're not in Kansas anymore.
Dan:	Good night!
SOUND:	**MUSICAL TRANSITION OUT OF SKETCH**
	(TERRY and LARRY exit after exchanging good-byes with DAN and JAN. DAN and JAN then continue . . .)
Dan:	Just think, we're going to get to spend an eternity with those two sweet youngsters.
Jan:	They're precious! Precious, I tell you.
Dan:	And I am so glad we could help them get a better grip on heaven.
Jan:	Me too.
Dan:	Impart our spiritual knowledge!
Jan:	Me too, dear.
	(Silence for a moment.)
Dan:	Did you have any idea what you were talking about?
Jan:	Not a clue! We have to get our Bible out and read it!
Dan:	Because I'm clearly getting my stories mixed up.
Jan:	Clearly is not the word for it . . .
	(MUSIC SWELLS)
	(DAN and JAN continue to converse, and as they begin to walk off . . .)
LIGHTS:	**FADE TO BLACK**
	END

▶ *Characterization:*
Jan & Dan Moment

Jan & Dan speak even when they are not talking: They are constantly nodding their heads and "mm-hmming" in agreement to whatever is being said. Develop little physical quirks that make them unique.

FRESH FRUIT

with Dan and Jan

TOPIC

Being a fruitful Christian

SYNOPSIS

A visit with Jan and Dan exposes their lack of knowledge about being a
fruitful Christian. When questioned by their guests about the importance of
bearing fruit, Dan and Jan take a moment or two to fully understand the
concept. After a bit of self-examination, Dan and Jan realize their spiritual
fruit is anything but fresh . . . it's rotten.

CHARACTERS

Dan – 30s to 40s; Christian; nerdish; overly reactive & nice

Jan – 30s to 40s, Dan's wife; nerdish; overly reactive & nice

Peter – New Christian

Kelly – Peter's wife; new Christian

SETS/PROPS

Sketch takes place in the living room of Dan and Jan's home: Chairs,
couch, coffee table. Props needed: Microphone on stand; karaoke machine;
bowl of fruit salad.

LIGHTS:	**BLACKOUT** *(Actors move into place)*
SOUND:	**MUSICAL TRANSITION INTO SKETCH**
GRAPHIC:	**TITLE SLIDE—** *FRESH FRUIT* with Dan & Jan
LIGHTS:	**UP ON STAGE**

(JAN and DAN are entertaining PETER and KELLY in the living room of their home. Next to the couch is a microphone on a stand next to a karaoke machine.)

(PETER and KELLY are sitting in chairs watching JAN and DAN, who are at the microphone singing the last notes of a song. PETER and KELLY applaud out of obligation. JAN and DAN improvise thank-you responses.)

Jan: For our next number, Dan and I would like to do yet another duet.

Dan: I thought I was going to do my song?

Jan: Oh, honey, you're right. It's time for your set. *(To the others)* You're going to love Dan's The Candy Man Can . . . he sounds just like Sammy.

Dan: Thank you, Jan, and then later you can do your Reba set.

Jan: *(With a bad Southern accent)* Okay!

Peter: Uh, hey, Kelly and I had no idea that you two loved to karaoke . . .

Kelly: We thought we were just coming over for dinner.

Peter: It's getting late, and we really had a few questions we wanted to ask you.

Jan: Oh, of course. We just get carried away.

Dan: We're frustrated performers.

Jan: Christian performers.

(JAN and DAN walk to the couch . . .)

Dan: Sometimes you just have to tell us, "Enough!"

Kelly: Last week at church you offered to answer any questions we had.

Jan: When Dan and I were new Christians we asked a lot of questions too, didn't we, honey?

Dan: I don't know. Did we?

(JAN and DAN laugh . . .)

You see, that was a question . . .

▸ *Drama Cue: Atmosphere*

When performing a sketch that's set in a specific location or different era, establish the mood with costumes, backdrop, and the appropriate music to carry your audience where you want them to go.

Jan:	You're killing me . . .
Peter:	Well do you mind if we ask you a question about something Kelly and I were discussing?
Jan:	As seasoned Christians it is our duty to help baby Christians with their first steps.
Kelly:	Good. We were wondering . . . we heard the pastor say that as Christians, we are to be fruitful.
Peter:	What does it mean for a Christian to bear good fruit?
	(JAN and DAN smile at each other . . . with a little giggling thrown in.)
Dan:	Oh, we get you.
Jan:	We see what's going on here.
Dan:	Well, yes . . . Jan and I know what bearing good fruit is all about! And their names are Spencer, Freida, Percy, and Pam.
Jan:	Would you like to meet them? They're upstairs cleaning out the fish tank. *(Turning and calling out)* Oh, Spencer . . .
Kelly:	No, no . . . we understand what that kind of "fruitful" means . . . .
Jan:	"Be fruitful and multiply!"
Kelly:	But isn't there another kind of fruit we are supposed to be concerned about?
Dan:	Oh . . . okay . . . I know what you're talking about. Well, first of all, no one knows for sure what kind of fruit was on the tree in the Garden of Eden. We just know it was a fruit!
Jan:	I have always believed it was an apple, but Dan . . .
Dan:	I have always felt strongly it was some type of fruit we can no longer purchase at the produce stand. A hybrid of, let's say a pineapple and a kumquat.
Jan:	But we know that Satan tempted Eve with the fruit.
Dan:	And then what did Eve do? She turned right around, and—I don't mean to offend you, Jan—but that woman tempted her husband, Adam. Which was wrong in my book.
Jan:	And honey, not to offend you, but if Adam were the spiritual leader he should have been in the Garden, he wouldn't have let that happen.
Peter:	Wait, we're not talking about the fruit in the Garden, or Adam and Eve. What we are trying to ask is, aren't we as Christians suppose to bear fruit? Spiritual fruit?
	(JAN and DAN look a little puzzled at first . . .)

▸ *Caution: Accents*

Use an accent if it will help establish your character, but never at the cost of articulation.

▸ *Characterization: Jan & Dan Moment*

Dan & Jan are sweet, but a little self-centered. The only time they think about others is when their guests bring them back to reality. So have their guests be direct with their questions about the Bible.

Dan:	Okay, you know, Jan, I think they're right. Yes, yes—we are supposed to bear fruit!
Kelly:	So what does that mean?
	(JAN and DAN are still a little perplexed . . .)
Dan:	Uh, Jan . . . go ahead . . .
Jan:	No, I think you should start . . . I'm thinking . . . thinking . . .
Dan:	Well it means we are to bear fruit . . . bear it . . . carry it . . . everywhere we go.
Jan:	Spiritual fruit!
Dan:	Yes! Spiritual fruit!
Jan:	Basketsful!
Peter:	But what is spiritual fruit? I mean, what are the fruits we are to bear?
Dan:	Okay, then, let's see . . . I think we should be bearing a plethora of fruits.
Jan:	Like a spiritual fruit salad of sorts.
Kelly:	The pastor said something about being a productive Christian. He mentioned witnessing, having a Christian testimony . . .
Peter:	And investing in the lives of other Christians at church.
Dan:	Very good. Well, there you have it.
Jan:	See how this all worked out?
Kelly:	So are we supposed to do all those things to bear spiritual fruit?
Jan:	That's right.
Peter:	Because Kelly and I are new Christians, can you tell us what you two do to bear fruit?
	(JAN and DAN are still a little perplexed . . .)
Dan:	Uh, well, we've done Chalk Talk at VBS . . .
Jan:	We headed up the puppet ministry!
Dan:	I was on the church carpet committee . . .
Jan:	I sang a solo . . . once . . .
Kelly:	So, that is producing fruit?
Jan:	Actually, we haven't done any of those things for over ten years . . .

▸ *Characterization:*
Jan & Dan Moment

No one else can make Jan laugh like Dan, and vice versa. So when the two interact, they should do so with passion and frivolity.

Dan:	We both have a sciatic nerve condition that . . .
Kelly:	We hate to get so personal, but Peter and I have noticed two different kinds of Christians. Christians who bear fruit, and Christians who don't.
Peter:	We just want to be fruit-bearing Christians . . . and we're trying to figure out how to make that happen.
Jan:	Well, kids, it is important to have fresh fruit.
Dan:	But wash it off first . . . . That was a joke.
	Everyone lets out an obligatory laugh.
Peter:	*(Standing)* Well, it's late and we'd better get going.
Kelly:	*(Standing)* You're right, dear.
Dan:	*(Standing)* But we haven't sung our tribute to Broadway yet!
Jan:	Yes, the karaoke machine just got warmed up!
Peter:	Maybe another time.
Kelly:	Thanks so much for taking the time to . . . uh. . . . answer our questions.
Jan:	Anytime, honey, anytime. And next time I'll make muffins . . . with fruit in them.
Peter:	We look forward to that. Let's go.
	(PETER and KELLY exit, improvising good-byes.)
Jan:	What a lovely couple!
Dan:	Honey, maybe we should have asked them to do a song with us. Do think that is why they left so abruptly?
Jan:	No. I think they left because we couldn't answer their questions about fruit.
Dan:	We don't have any spiritual fruit, do we?
Jan:	We do, but it isn't fresh!
Dan:	It's ten years old and rotten!
Jan:	Flies everywhere!
SOUND:	**MUSICAL TRANSITION OUT OF SKETCH**
Dan:	Well, I don't mean to offend you, Jan, but you're the one who used to complain about the VBS Chalk Talks and the puppet ministry . . .

▶ *Characterization: Jan & Dan Moment*

When Jan & Dan begin preaching, have them speak with authority. Though they are mixing up Scripture, in their minds their theology is right-on.

Jan: And I don't mean to offend you, Dan, but as head of this household you should have put your foot down. You're just like Adam . . .

(JAN and DAN continue their discussion as . . . .)

LIGHTS: **FADE TO BLACK**

    END

Plan B

At home with Jan and Dan

TOPIC
Faith

SYNOPSIS
Jan and Dan are once again entertaining friends from church.
When their friends ask questions about faith, Jan and Dan totally
confuse them. As is always the case with Dan and Jan, they wind up
doing more harm than good.

CHARACTERS

Dan – overly polite, sweet and helpful; husband to Jan

Jan – overly polite, sweet and helpful; wife to Dan

Robert – single; 20s

Tasha – single; 20s

SETS/PROPS

Couch

Tray of Rice Krispie Treats

Two chairs

Coffee mugs

Coffee table

A few board games

LIGHTS:	**BLACKOUT** *(Actors move into place)*
SOUND:	**MUSICAL TRANSITION INTO SKETCH**
GRAPHIC:	**TITLE SLIDE—** *Plan B* At home with Dan and Jan
LIGHTS:	**UP ON STAGE**

(We see the living room of DAN and JAN's home. TASHA and ROBERT sit in chairs on each side of the sofa. DAN sits on the couch. JAN stands behind the couch with a tray of treats and a few mugs)

Dan: I am so glad you two youngsters dropped by tonight!

Jan: You have blessed us with your presence! Haven't they, dear?

Dan: Our blessers are full and running over!

Jan: *(Moving to sit on the couch next to DAN)* Running over!

Robert: Well, thanks for letting us stop by on such short notice.

Tasha: After the singles' Bible study, Robert and I had a few questions and, well, it seems like so many people come to you when they have questions about the Bible.

Robert: A lot of people look up to you two.

Jan: They do?

Dan: *(Pointing to JAN)* That's because of this one right here! She is precious in His sight, I tell you—and my sight as well.

Jan: *(Pointing back to DAN)* You. You're the rock in this house!

Dan: It's you!

Jan: No, it's you!

Dan: Don't believe her for a moment! Jan has a way of bringing whatever it is back to the spiritual! Like these treats she made.

Jan: *(Holding up the platter)* Bible Rice Krispie Treats!

Dan: See. What did I tell you?

Tasha: Bible Rice Krispie Treats?

Jan: *(Pointing to the different cookies)* this one is in the shape of the Ark. And here we have the Tower of Babel! A camel, a flock of sheep . . .

Dan: Amazing. You should have your own show.

Jan: What did you say?

Dan: I said you should have your own show.

▸ *Characterization:*
Jan & Dan Moment

Reality sets in after Jan & Dan's guests leave. There is a point in their dialogue when they realize they haven't a clue what they were talking about . . . this is the drama's serious moment. But as soon as Dan & Jan recognize and admit it, they go back to being their syrupy sweet selves.

Jan:	You are the kindest, sweetest thing this side of heaven . . .
	(JAN and DAN continue to compliment each other)
Robert:	Actually, we didn't come here to eat; we came here to ask you a very important question.
Tasha:	We're having trouble grasping the concept of something that is supposed to be the foundation of our faith.
Dan:	And what would that be?
Robert:	Faith. What is faith?
Tashsa:	Can you to tell us what faith is?
	(DAN and JAN are a little puzzled. They don't know exactly what to say.)
Dan:	Faith.
Jan:	Faith.
Dan:	You did say faith?
Jan:	That's what they said, dear.
Dan:	Well, uh, Jan, why don't you take this one?
Jan:	I seem to be drawing big fat zeros on this one. Zeros . . . zeros . . .
Dan:	Okay, faith. Faith is something you cannot see . . .
Jan:	That's right! It's invisible.
Dan:	But it is all around you.
Jan:	It's like air. It's there, but you can't see it. Unless, of course, you live in Los Angeles . . .
Dan:	And as I recall, without faith it is impossible to play God!
Jan:	No, honey. I think it is impossible to "please" God.
Dan:	Oh. What did I say?
Jan:	You said "play" God. It's *please* God . . . but it was cute, honey. Cute!
Robert:	Someone told us that faith is trusting God.
Jan:	Now, whoever told you that gave you a nugget right there!
Tasha:	So, how do we put that into practice?
Robert:	Yeah, Jan and Dan. How do you two put faith into practice in your lives?
	(Puzzled again, stammering)
Dan:	Well, you . . . step out in faith!

▶ *Characterization: Jan & Dan Moment*

Jan & Dan love to feel like they are helping others. So no matter how mixed-up the two get about important details, they really strive to make their knowledge benefit their guests. When it sounds good, they are really proud of themselves!

Jan:	Step out like you've never stepped before!
Dan:	You . . . pray by faith.
Jan:	I'm thinking that there is . . . uh . . . blind faith—though you need to know that you could get hurt very badly from that one.
	(Again looking at each other for help)
Robert:	So, you trust God . . .
Tasha:	Pray about it . . .
Robert:	Then step out by faith!
Dan:	Right. And always have a Plan B.
Tasha:	A Plan B?
Jan:	Oh yes. You never can be too sure how things are going to turn out. So be ready to have another plan in case *(pointing upward)* doesn't come through.
Robert:	I don't see how you are to live by faith if you have an optional Plan B ready.
Dan:	Things don't always turn out the way you want them to.
Tasha:	But if you trust God, shouldn't you accept how He answers your prayers?
Dan:	Okay, I see what you're getting at. But even though God may be in the driver's seat, it is sure nice to have a passenger side spiritual airbag just in case!
Jan:	God may be my umbrella, but I always carry that little plastic rain bonnet in my purse!
Dan:	I may be trusting God to power that Walkman of spiritual joy that's playing in my life, but I always keep an extra battery in my pocket!
Jan:	I'll follow God's recipe, but I have store-bought in the freezer just in case!
Robert:	But how can you have faith and really not have . . . faith?
Dan:	Faith is like sitting on a chair . . . *(loses line of illustration)* . . . I lost my train of thought . . .
Jan:	You were saying faith is like sitting on a chair . . .
Dan:	Right . . . right. You may have never sat in that chair before, but you just believe that when you sit on that chair . . . no one else is going to get to sit there.
Jan:	And it will be warm when the next person sits down!
Dan:	Beautiful, honey. Beautiful!

▸ *Drama Cue: Tempo*

When performing a drama with multiple transitions, it's important to keep the pace moving. Transitions can slow down a sketch. Maintain a steady tempo, keep the dialogue flowing smoothly, and move the action along.

Tasha:	*(Very confused)* I think it's time to go, Robert.
Robert:	*(Standing)* Yeah, it's late.
	(Everyone stands)
Tasha:	Thanks for your time.
Dan:	That's what we're here for.
Robert:	So, as older Christians talking to new Christians, you're telling us that we can have faith in God, even while we have a Plan B to get what we want just in case He doesn't come through the way we expect Him to?
Dan:	You're a quick learner! Isn't he?
Jan:	You should be a preacher, I tell you! That was good, the way you put that all together.
Tasha:	Good night.
Robert:	Thank you, Dan and Jan.
Dan:	Anytime.
	(ROBERT and TASHA exit)
SOUND:	**MUSICAL TRANSITION OUT OF SKETCH**
Jan:	Precious, aren't they?
Dan:	Precious in His sight.
Jan:	God is really using us in our church . . .
Dan:	Sharing our wisdom on faith . . .
Jan:	And about always having a Plan B ready . . . just in case!
Dan:	*(Snaps his fingers)* I meant to tell them, "When the rubber meets the road, have faith in God, but make sure you are carrying a spare!"
Jan:	Or, "I'm trusting God to clothe me in righteousness, but I always keep that emergency sewing kit in my purse!"
Dan:	You are amazing!
Jan:	We're amazing!
	(They sit and begin eating the Rice Krispie Treats . . .)
LIGHTS:	**FADE TO BLACK**
	END

▸ *Characterization: Jan & Dan Moment*

Every Jan & Dan drama contains a bit of dialogue that gives the audience a peek into their lovesick relationship. Have fun with this section, then move on to the message of the drama.

▸ *Caution: Hand Props*

Don't wait until the performance to use hand props—it will distract the actors. Make sure they practice with their hand props during all rehearsals. (This is especially crucial for a prop-intensive drama.)

THE QUITTERS' ACQUITTAL

with Jan and Dan

TOPIC
Quitting: Can we come back to God and spiritual things once we've quit?

SCRIPTURE
Acts 15:36-41 / Colossians 4:10 / 2 Timothy 4:11

SYNOPSIS
Jan and Dan are having their day in "Quitters' Court." Appearing before a judge, Jan and Dan answer a string of questions that prove Jan and Dan have never completed anything they started. They are guilty of quitting in the first degree. Most of their wrongs can't be made right, but there is one area of their lives where they hope they can have a second chance.

CHARACTERS

Dan – overly polite; nervous; helpful; husband to Jan

Jan – overly polite; sweet; nervous; helpful; wife to Dan

Judge – not seen, only heard, serious, strong, but compassionate

PROPS

Sketch takes place in a courtroom, though a courtroom set is not needed. Three posters need to be made:

Poster 1: "Exhibit A" – Dan's Allergies
(Glued to poster board are different types of plants Dan is allergic to)

Poster 2: "Exhibit B" – Jan's Careers
(Glued to the poster board are photos of the various careers and interests Jan has pursued)

Poster 3: "Exhibit C" – Jan's Arts & Crafts
(Pictures and word labels of the different arts and crafts Jan has tried: macramé, decoupage, ceramics, puffy paints, the BeDazzler, etc.)

LIGHTS:	**BLACKOUT** *(Actors move into place)*
SOUND:	**MUSICAL TRANSITION INTO SKETCH**
GRAPHIC:	**QUITTER'S COURT** *Case #914: The Quitters' Acquittal*
LIGHTS:	**UP ON STAGE**

(We see an empty stage. The stage is dark around the sides and brighter at center stage)

Note:	Judge is never seen, only heard. Jan and Dan direct their attention out toward the audience as if facing the judge's bench.
Judge:	Case number 914. The case of Jan and Dan. Jan and Dan, please approach the bench.

(Jan and Dan nervously enter and stand center stage in the pool of light. Jan carries two poster boards and Dan carries one. Jan and Dan are very apprehensive about their courtroom date.)

Dan:	Hello, I'm Dan.
Jan:	And I'm Jan.
Judge:	Are you both aware of the charges that brought you to Quitter's Court today?
Dan:	Yes sir.
Jan:	Yes siree.
Judge:	And can you tell the court what you are being charged for?
Dan:	We are quitters.
Jan:	Apparently we have a long string of charges related to the fact that we have a tendency to quit.
Judge:	And how do you plead?
Dan:	Well, I'll tell you . . .
Jan:	. . . we're not sure . . .
Dan:	. . . there are extenuating circumstances . . .
Jan:	. . . we'd like to explain . . .
Dan:	. . . we made posters . . .
Jan:	*(slightly turning to the side)* . . . I brought my best friend along as a character witness . . .
Judge:	Guilty or not guilty?
Jan and Dan:	Not guilty.
Judge:	Not guilty? You have a lot of charges here. Dan, let's start with you.

▸ *Drama Cue:*
Typecasting

Because a pantomime contains no dialogue, initial impressions speak louder than words. Typecasting for a pantomime will help your audience believe the characters are who they are supposed to be.

▸ *Characterization:*
Jan & Dan Moment

Jan & Dan's signs should reflect their image: Be sure their "exhibits" look like they arrived from the past with them!

(DAN steps forward as JAN takes a step back; the following questioning from the judge goes quickly like in a fast-paced courtroom drama)

You have a long record of quitting.

Dan: I do, but I have reasons.

Judge: As a child, you quit swimming lessons.

Dan: Earaches.

Judge: Boy Scouts?

Dan: I couldn't tie a square knot.

Judge: Soccer?

Dan: Weak ankles.

Judge: In junior high, you backed out of the school play an hour before curtain on opening night.

Dan: It was a dumb play.

Judge: The play was "You're a Good Man, Charlie Brown."

Dan: Yes. Yes, that was it. I didn't have a very big role anyway.

Judge: What role did you have?

Dan: Charlie Brown. *(Scrunches up his face)* Stage fright!

Judge: Let's see here, you took up golfing and quit. Baseball and quit. Tennis and quit.

Dan: True, but I've got allergies. *(Turns poster around)* As you'll see here on the chart I've prepared, I am allergic to ragweed, dandelions, Bermuda grass . . .

Judge: That will be enough, Dan.

Dan: I had to have my tonsils and adenoids removed . . .

Judge: Thank you, Dan. Jan, please step forward.

(DAN steps back and JAN steps forward. As they pass each other they dramatically mouth "I love you" as if they were in a serious courtroom drama)

Jan, you are a quitter, too.

Jan: Yes. Yes, I am, but I, too, have reasons . . .

Judge: We'll start with your childhood. Your parents gave you riding lessons . . . but you quit.

Jan: I wasn't real fond of how the horses smelled.

▸ *Caution: Overacting*

When actors perform pantomime, they often exaggerate gestures and facial expressions to compensate for absence of dialogue. Their movements should be precise, deliberate, and choreographed. However, avoid overacting: It makes characters clownish and corny.

Judge:	You tried ice skating, and you quit.
Jan:	I've struggled with motion sickness since I was a child.
Judge:	Quit ballet.
Jan:	I was accidentally injuring the other swans.
Judge:	As an adult, you've had how many careers?
Jan:	Well, at least six.
Judge:	You quit them all.
Jan:	*(Turning her first poster around and pointing to the various pictures)* As you will see here, I tried supermodeling and the cutthroat world of fast food; I was a trucker for six weeks; I was a waitress . . . but had carpal tunnel . . .
Judge:	And quit them all. Just like all the arts and crafts projects you started, then quit.
Jan:	*(Turning her second poster around)* But I had nothing else left to BeDazzle in my closet . . .
Judge:	You quit them all! Is that true?
Jan:	True.
Judge:	Is it true that you both have quit exercising?
	(DAN walks forward and stands next to JAN, taking hold of her hand)
Jan & Dan:	Yes.
Judge:	Quit brushing between meals?
Jan & Dan:	Yes.
Judge:	Quit the PTA and the YMCA.
Jan & Dan:	Yes.
Judge:	And above all, you've quit church . . . quit taking an interest in spiritual things altogether.
	(JAN and DAN drop their heads)
	I find you guilty of all charges. No telling what your lives would have been like today had you only stuck with something instead of quitting.
Dan:	And our punishment?
Judge:	Because you can't go back and change what's already been done, you'll live with regret. I think that's punishment enough.
Jan:	Judge, I know that we can't go back and change the past. But there is one area where we ask for your mercy and would like a clean start.

▸ *Characterization: Jan & Dan Moment*

Jan & Dan are not in their home in this sketch; they are in a courtroom. Though they are away from their comfort zone, they should behave in vintage Jan & Dan form.

Judge:	What's that?
Jan:	Spiritual things.
Dan:	We've made mistakes in our Christian walk. Been discouraged! We quit trusting God. Stopped going to church and even quit reading our Bibles.
Jan:	Does God have it in **His** heart to forgive us, and to give a couple of quitters a second chance?
Judge:	When you pass up a chance in life to succeed by quitting, you usually can't ever go back and make it up. But from what I read in the Word of God, our heavenly Father is always ready to give quitters another chance.
Dan:	Even those with bad ankles?
Jan:	And motion sickness?
Judge:	Yes, and even those who've given up on what God wants them to do with their lives. Now, if you'll leave here today and get back to doing what God wants you to do, I'll drop all the charges.
SOUND:	**MUSICAL TRANSITION OUT OF SKETCH**
Dan:	We'll do it!
Jan:	We've quit being quitters! Right, honey?
Dan:	Right. *(Looking up for the Judge's approval)* It *is* okay to quit quitting, isn't it?
	(JAN and DAN nervously await the JUDGE's response)
Judge:	Quitters acquitted! Case dismissed!
	(JAN and DAN hug at the news of the good verdict)
LIGHTS:	**AFTER A FEW SECONDS ... FADE TO BLACK**
	END

▶ *Characterization: Jan & Dan Moment*

Don't overcreate the secondary roles in this sketch. Jan & Dan dramas are about Jan & Dan; the supporting characters exist solely to make Jan & Dan all the more outrageous.

THE PROVERBIAL MARRIAGE

with Jan & Dan

TOPIC

Marriage: What the book of Proverbs has to say about a successful marriage relationship.

SYNOPSIS

A young couple comes to visit Jan and Dan just weeks before their wedding. The couple hopes to glean some advice about marriage from Jan and Dan, only to leave a little more confused about what the Bible has to say about marriage.

CHARACTERS

Dan – middle-aged; Jan's husband; Christian; nerdish; backward; too proper

Jan – middle-aged; Dan's wife; Christian; nerdish; backward; too proper

Glenn – young man; Sarah's fiancé

Sarah – young woman; Glenn's fiancée

SETS/PROPS

Sketch takes place in the living room of Jan and Dan's home. Props that are needed: Wedding album, wedding invitation, game of Twister, cheerleading pom-poms

LIGHTS:	**BLACKOUT** *(Actors move into positions)*
SOUND:	**MUSICAL TRANSITION INTO SKETCH**
GRAPHIC:	**TITLE SLIDE—** *The Proverbial Marriage*
LIGHTS:	**UP ON STAGE**

(DAN, GLENN, and SARAH are standing in the living room as JAN enters with a tray of hot chocolate)

Jan: Alrighty . . . who would like some cocoa? Time for hot cocoa!

Dan: Oh, looky here! Jan made hot chocolate! Isn't she amazing?

Sarah: She sure is.

Glenn: *(Taking a cup)* Thank you, Jan!

Jan: You are certainly welcome. Yes, siree! Shall I pop some popcorn?

Sarah: Oh, no thank you!

Glenn: No, ma'am.

Dan: We could make popcorn balls! We love to make popcorn balls, don't we, Jan?

Jan: We certainly do. And make faces on them with M&M's.

Sarah: No, really. This is fine.

Jan: *(Sitting)* Well, we are just tickled pink that you two stopped by tonight. Aren't we, honey?

Dan: If we were any pinker, we'd be red!

Glenn: Well, as you know, Sarah and I are getting married in three weeks.

Sarah: And someone at church thought you might give us some words of wisdom about marriage before our wedding day.

Dan: *(In a very loud and serious voice)* Don't do it!

(SARAH and GLENN are shocked)

Jan: He's kidding! He's a kidder!

Dan: *(Laughing)* I'm just kidding you two youngsters!

Glenn: You scared me there for a moment.

Dan: *(Once again very loud and serious)* You *should* be scared!

(SARAH and GLENN are once again taken aback)

▶ *Drama Cue: Variety*

When you have a cast made up of similar kinds of people, assign each of the characters a distinct trait—a specific mannerism, costume, speech pattern, etc. A good script will offer clues to every character's individuality.

Jan:	He's kidding again! He's a big kidder!
Dan:	Just kidding you before the big day!
Sarah:	Okay, then. Could you tell us the secret of your good marriage?
Jan:	Well, honey, our marriage is not a secret! Why, we had over nineteen people at our wedding. *(Taking the wedding album off the table)* We even have pictures to prove that we got married. That's me in the white dress.
Dan:	And that's me singing to my bride "Love is a Many-Splintered Thing."
Jan:	Honey, no. The name of the song is "Love Is a Many-Splendored Thing."
Dan:	What did I say?
Jan:	You said "splintered thing." Splintered! But it was cute!
Dan:	Splendored. Splintered. A little bit of both! Right, honey?
Jan:	You're a rascal! A rascal you are!
Sarah:	*(Looking at book)* Your pictures are very nice.
Jan:	Look there. We served popcorn balls at the reception!
Dan:	A full popcorn ball buffet!
Glenn:	I think what Sarah was asking was, what does it take to have a successful marriage?
Jan:	Oh, I get you.
Dan:	Well, it takes a man and woman.
Jan:	Very important place to start.
Dan:	A proposal.
Jan:	A ring.
Dan:	A date.
Jan:	A dress.
Dan:	Her family.
Jan:	His family.
Dan:	"I do!"
Jan:	"I do!"
Dan:	Some cake.

▸ *Characterization: Jan & Dan Moment*

Jan & Dan Moment: There comes a moment in every Jan & Dan sketch when their guests finally realize that this conversation is going nowhere! At that point they should initiate their exit by standing and bringing the conversation to a close. Ever cordial, Jan & Dan always oblige

Jan:	Red punch!
Dan:	Bad Salisbury steak!
Jan:	And bingo!
Jan & Dan:	Man and wife!
Jan:	Isn't it great how it all comes together? More cocoa?
Sarah:	But anyone can get married. We want to know what it takes to have a great marriage relationship.
Dan:	Oh? Okay. I see.
Jan:	Okay. I see what you are getting at. Apparently our secret has gotten around the church, Dan.
Dan:	Apparently so.
Jan:	Well, if you must know . . . *(She reaches under the couch and pulls out the game of Twister)* Here it is! Twister!
Glenn:	Twister?
Dan:	This game has saved our marriage!
Sarah:	You've got to be kidding!
Jan:	Right hand: blue!
Dan:	Left foot: green!
Jan & Dan:	*(in unison)* Let nothing evil come between!
Sarah:	Twister? Is that it? This is all the wisdom you have for us concerning marriage?
Jan:	You can dress alike! That's always fun!
Dan:	It helps you spot each other in a crowd faster!
Jan:	And have plenty of His and Hers towels on hand. His and Hers towels are very unifying, you know!
Dan:	And leave each other notes. I found this note in my lunch box today. *(Pulls note from pocket)* It says, "Remember to pick up the dry cleaning." Isn't that the sweetest thing you ever heard? She's a gem!
Jan:	*You're* a gem!
Glenn:	I guess what Sarah and I are looking for is wisdom on marriage from the Bible.
Dan:	The Bible?

▶ *Caution: Gentle with Genders*

Dialogue in an all-male or all-female cast can come off as "bashing" the opposite sex. Make sure that any lines about the opposite gender are delivered in an innocent, inoffensive way.

Jan:	Oh, the Bible.
Sarah:	We figure your relationship is based on the biblical definition of love.
Jan:	Well, it is. We know that love is patient, love is kind. Love is . . .
Dan:	. . . love is in the air . . .
Jan:	Love is a many-splendored thing!
Dan:	Love makes the world go round!
Glenn:	We've been reading the book of Proverbs and found that Solomon said a lot about love.
Dan:	Proverbs? I mean, yes, Proverbs.
Jan:	Solomon? I mean, yes, Solomon.
Sarah:	Honey, isn't it getting a little late?
Glenn:	Yeah. *(Standing)* We should be going.
	(Everyone stands)
Sarah:	Thanks for having us over.
Jan:	Anytime. Oh, and . . . *(Reaches behind the coach and takes out a wrapped wedding present. It is the exact same size as the game of Twister on the table)* . . . here is a little wedding present for the two of you. *(She hands it to SARAH)*
Dan:	*(Picking up the game of Twister on the table)* I bet you can't guess what it is!
	(SARAH and GLENN laugh nervously)
Glenn:	Thank you.
Jan:	See you on the big day! 'Bye.
	(GLENN and SARAH exit)
Dan:	Cute kids, huh? So what do you say? A game of Twister?
Jan:	*(Not interested)* No. *(Another idea)* Want to go look at our His and Hers towel collection?
Dan:	Nah. Want to dress alike?
Jan:	Nah. Popcorn balls?
Dan:	Nah.
	(JAN and DAN sit on the couch together. They look very bored. Then, after a moment . . .)

▸ *Characterization: Jan & Dan Moment*

Hand props should match their owners. Jan & Dan should have distinctive household accessories that parallel their retro life. Inexpensive vintage looking props can be found in most department stores. Better yet, start by looking in secondhand or resale stores.

Jan:	Do you think it's about time we crack that Bible open?
Dan:	Proverbs?
Jan:	Yes!
Dan:	I'll get the Bible.
Jan:	I'll make the popcorn balls!
SOUND:	**MUSICAL TRANSITION OUT OF SKETCH**
	(JAN and DAN hold hands and as they exit the stage ...)
LIGHTS:	**FADE TO BLACK**
	END

▶ *Characterization:*
Jan & Dan Moment

Jan & Dan always want to appear perfect, without any chinks to be found in their armor. So direct them to be overly pretentious and self-adulatory.

Beware! Ready or Not!
IT'S GUS & GLADYS!

We've all known someone just like them: They show up late and leave early. They've worn the same clothes for years but are always asking everyone else to change. They don't agree on anything except that YOU bug them! Though it appears every minute Gus & Gladys spend together is pure torture, they've been married for thirty-odd "wonderful" years.

Gus & Gladys are blunt, rude, and crusty—but lovable from the top of their heads to the tip of their toes. Your audience will cheer every time they show their wrinkled faces! Why? Because underneath their tough exterior, Gus & Gladys are nothing but pussycats!

Here are a few Drama Cues to help you produce the sketches featuring Gus & Gladys:

Image

In their midfifties, Gus & Gladys are somewhat physically challenged. They are a little hunched over, they walk with some effort, and neither knows a thing about correct posture. They lean, shift their weight from side to side, and can't talk without emphasizing their words with body language. In a nutshell, they need to work out and clean up!

Wardrobe

Gus & Gladys wear the same clothes every time they show up. Your audience should never see them in anything but the same moth-eaten clothes they wear with penny-pinching pride.

Gladys is a double-knit fan: Put her in a hideous dress with exposed knee-highs. Have her wear an old wool jacket no matter what she is doing or what season it is. And Gladys never leaves home without her purse!

Gus is old-school—double-knit sport coat, wide tie, and polyester dress pants. He talks through his moustache and peers through black-rimmed glasses. Some say Gus looks like your high school shop teacher, but to me, he looks like the crusty old guy that failed you on your first driving test!

Paul's Favorites

Because everyone has a Gus & Gladys in their life, they provide a welcome bit of comedy relief. I never get tired of creating dramas that feature them. The following are my favorite Gus & Gladys sketches and the *Life Scripts* volumes they can be found in:

Close Encounters of the Married Kind / *Life Scripts for the Church: Characters*
Sitting in Judgment / *Life Scripts for the Church: Characters*
The Most Wonderful Time of the Year / *Life Scripts for the Church: Holidays*

Want some ideas about what Gus & Gladys might look like? Check out photos of the original cranky couple at www.pauljoiner.com and meet Gus & Gladys!

And now, Gus & Gladys!

CLOSE ENCOUNTERS OF THE MARRIED KIND

with Gus and Gladys Glum

TOPIC
Marriage/Submission

SCRIPTURE
Ephesians 5:22-33

SYNOPSIS
Gus and Gladys Glum attend a Couples Encounter Weekend to focus on strengthening their marriage. Gus and Gladys are very uncooperative during the group exercises, particularly the one on submission. Gus and Gladys eventually cause rifts between all the other couples; by the end of the session, theirs is the only relationship left intact.

SETS/PROPS
Two clipboards are required, but no particular set is needed. Sketch can take place indoors or outdoors. Chairs or benches are optional.

CHARACTERS

Buddy Darling – facilitator of Couples Encounter Weekend; husband to Samantha

Samantha Darling – facilitator of Couples Encounter Weekend; wife to Buddy

Chad Stone – young; newly married; husband to Kirstie

Kirstie Stone – young; newly married; wife to Chad

Gus Glum – opinionated; stubborn; impatient; husband to Gladys

Gladys Glum – harsh; severe, insecure; wife to Gus

LIGHTS:	**BLACKOUT** *(Actors move into place)*
SOUND:	**MUSICAL TRANSITION INTO SKETCH**
GRAPHIC:	**TITLE SLIDE—** *Close Encounters of the Married Kind*
LIGHTS:	**UP ON STAGE**

(BUDDY and SAMANTHA are greeting CHAD and KIRSTIE. BUDDY and SAMANTHA are wearing matching polo shirts, which helps the audience recognize them as staff employees. They each carry a clipboard. CHAD and KIRSTIE should also be dressed alike.)

Buddy: Good morning! I'm Buddy . . .

Samantha: . . . and I'm Samantha.

Buddy: And we want to welcome you two to Couples Encounter Weekend. *(Looking at his clipboard)* Now, you two are . . .

Chad: Chad and Kirstie Stone.

Buddy: Yes, the Stones. *(Checking them off his list)*

Samantha: You seem like a very lovely couple!

Kirstie: We think so!

Buddy: We are expecting another couple to participate with us today, but apparently they're a no-show.

(GUS and GLADYS enter, late as usual. And as usual they are irritable.)

Gus: Sorry we're late! Gladys went ballistic on me during the trip up here!

Gladys: That's because you wouldn't stop at a rest area! After Gus passed the sixteenth rest area and still wouldn't stop, I had to bail out of our moving car as we approached the seventeenth! I figured he'd have to come back for me.

Gus: The only reason I turned the car around and came back to get you was because the pecan log I bought at Stuckey's was still in your purse!

Buddy: *(Trying to lighten the moment)* You must be the Glums.

Gus: *(Still agitated)* Gus Glum. This is my wife, Gladys. Say hello, Gladys.

Gladys: Hello.

Samantha: Well, welcome to Couples Encounter Weekend. My husband, Buddy, and I are the directors here, and we know we are going to have a wonderful weekend together working on strengthening our marriages.

▶ *Drama Cue: Object Lesson*

When a drama is written around specific props, what you are performing is an object lesson. Each prop featured in a script represents something specific. Actors should understand that the props are every bit as meaningful as their dialogue.

Buddy:	Chad, Kirstie, why are you here this weekend?
Chad:	Today is our first anniversary.
Kirstie:	And we don't want the honeymoon to end! So, we're here to learn how to love each other even more.
Buddy:	Gus and Gladys?
Gus:	We won the tickets in a raffle at the mobile home improvement show.
Gladys:	It was free. We thought we'd check it out.
Buddy:	Well, it's great to have both of you couples here.
Samantha:	Now, feel free to be yourselves. In fact, if you'd like to call each other by your pet names, we encourage you to. For instance, I call Buddy "Scruffy"!
Buddy:	And I call Samantha "Sunshine"!
Kirstie:	I call Chad "He-Man." And he calls me "Snuggle-Blossom"!
Buddy:	Gus, do have a nickname for Gladys?
Gus:	*(Pauses for a moment)* I affectionately call Gladys . . . "Woman"!
Gladys:	*(Spiteful)* And I don't think I should tell you what I call Gus!
Buddy:	Okay then, moving along. Let's start off with a communication exercise.
Samantha:	Because most couples do not communicate well! Right, Scruffy?
Buddy:	Right, Sunshine! Now, let's start with Chad and Kirstie. I'd like both of you to face each other. Chad, close your eyes and when I count to three, open your eyes, look at your wife, and tell her what you see! Ready? One, two, three!
Chad:	*(Opens his eyes)* I see a beautiful woman! I see my lifetime companion! My best friend! My wife!
Kirstie:	That's the sweetest thing you've ever said to me!
	(CHAD and KIRSTIE embrace)
Buddy:	Great!
Samantha:	Now Gus, it's your turn. Face Gladys and close your eyes. Now, open them! What do you see?
	(GUS opens his eyes and looks at GLADYS. GLADYS is posturing, giving Gus the "evil eye," as if to say, "You'd better be careful what you say!")
Gus:	*(Hesitating)* I see Gladys. My wife. The mother of my children. The cooker of my meals. The cleaner of my house. The massager of my feet.
	(The other couples are shocked)

▸ *Caution: Prop Shop*

When the foundation of a sketch is its props, do everything in your power to find the right ones. Last-minute searches usually turn up items that are not functional, believable, or professional; this will kill a prop-specific drama. Take the time to prop shop!

Gladys:	*(Pats her purse ... like a gunslinger)* And don't forget the keeper of your pecan log! So you'd better watch it, or you'll never see your pecan log again!
Buddy:	*(Changing the subject)* Okay. Time to move on!
Samantha:	Everyone did a good job with the last exercise. Now we're going to focus on an area where couples seem to have problems.
Buddy & **Samantha:**	*(in unison)* Submission.
Buddy:	Let's do some submission exercises!
Gus:	Just a minute! If you think Gladys and I are going to take part in some touchy-feely, warm-and-fuzzy sensitive training submission exercises, you've got another thing coming!
Gladys:	We're Christians!
Buddy:	Well, the Bible speaks about submission.
Gus:	The Bible talks about fire and brimstone too, but that doesn't mean I want it! Anyway, I'm the head of the house . . . I call the shots!
Samantha:	But that's not the attitude you should have. You should both prefer one another.
Gus:	That's right. And I prefer that I call the shots and Gladys listens.
Kirstie:	That is so unfair!
Samantha:	We've got a lot of work to do!
Buddy:	Now take it easy, ladies. Technically, Gus has a point.
Samantha:	Are you sticking up for Gus?
	(Debate should gradually grow heated)
Buddy:	No, but ultimately he is responsible.
Chad:	That's right.
Kirstie:	That's right? You're buying all of this?
Chad:	Kirstie, Gus *is* the man of the house.
Kirstie:	And Gladys is the *woman* of the house!
Samantha:	Preach it, sister!
Buddy:	Samantha, what are you acting like this for? What kind of an example are you setting for these couples?
Gus:	Yeah, what kind of example are you setting for my wife?
Chad:	Or my wife!
Kirstie:	I'm finding out all sorts of things I never knew about you!

▸ *Characterization:*
Gus & Gladys Moment

Gus & Gladys's marriage sounds torturous, but they are truly in love. Who else could they find to put up with them? Though Gus & Gladys have their moments of bickering, be sure your audience also sees moments of affection. This will accentuate their love for each other, rather than focusing on just the disdain.

Gladys:	See what you've done? Now Cutesie is upset!
Kirstie:	It's Kirstie!
Buddy:	All right, enough. Samantha, let it go! Consider that an order.
Samantha:	A *what*?
Kirstie:	Don't let him talk to you that way!
Chad:	You should stay out of it . . . and that's an order!
Kirstie:	Excuse me?
Samantha:	We don't need to listen to this! C'mon, Kirstie, let's get out of here! We'll take our van!
	(SAMANTHA & KIRSTIE ad-lib dialogue as they exit stage . . .)
Buddy:	Go ahead. Whatever!
Chad:	Yeah, we'll beat you down the mountain! *(TO BUDDY)* We can take my Blazer!
	(BUDDY and CHAD exit together, leaving GUS and GLADYS onstage)
SOUND:	**TRANSITION MUSIC OUT OF SKETCH**
Gus:	Well, Gladys, I told you we'd be the best couple up here this weekend. It looks like we've got a pretty good thing going, you and me, don't we?
Gladys:	*(Unenthusiastic)* Yes, dear.
Gus:	Since we're all the way up here, why don't we make a day of it? Let's just sit back and enjoy the beauty of this mountain and eat that pecan log!
Gladys:	*(Pulling the pecan log out of her purse and handing it to GUS . . .)* Anything you say, Gus. Anything you say.
LIGHTS:	**FADE TO BLACK**
	END

▸ *Characterization:*
Gus & Gladys Moment

Gus & Gladys always arrive late in a sketch. Let your audience hear the cranky couple coming before they actually arrive. Rehearse some ad-lib dialogue between Gus & Gladys that they can use as "traveling" conversation. Chances are, Gus is telling Gladys to "hurry it up!"

Sitting in Judgment

with Gus and Gladys Glum

TOPIC
Judging others

SCRIPTURE
Matthew 7:1-6

SYNOPSIS
Gus and Gladys Glum join another couple for lunch out at a cafe. During lunch, Gus and Gladys watch another couple sitting at a nearby table and begin to speculate as to who they are and what they are like. Judging solely by appearance, they assume this couple is worldly and wild. The Glums are surprised when the couple prays over their meal . . . and they immediately switch gears, believing that they are now seeing a religious display.

SETS/PROPS
Cafe setting: 1 table; 4 chairs; tablecloth and table settings/centerpiece. Glasses. Menus. Waiter will need a pad of paper, a pen, and a serving tray.

CHARACTERS
Waiter

Robert Maines – friend of Glums; husband to Gloria

Gloria Maines – friend of Glums; wife to Robert

Gus Glum – opinionated; stubborn; impatient; husband to Gladys

Gladys Glum – harsh; severe; insecure; wife to Gus

LIGHTS:	**BLACKOUT** *(Actors move into place)*
SOUND:	**MUSIC TRANSITION INTO SKETCH**
GRAPHIC:	**TITLE SLIDE—** *Sitting In Judgment*
LIGHTS:	**UP ON CAFE**

(ROBERT and GLORIA sit at a table looking at their menus. WAITER enters and walks to them . . .)

Waiter: Do you care to go ahead and order, or do you still want to wait for the rest of your party?

Robert: I think we'll wait.

Gloria: They should be here any minute . . . they must be running a little late.

Waiter: All right, I'll come back.

(GUS and GLADYS enter . . . they look a little irritated.)

Gloria: *(Seeing GUS and GLADYS)* Oh . . . Gus, Gladys, over here.

Robert: *(Standing)* You made it. We were worried you had forgotten about lunch.

Gus: We are late because Gladys here couldn't find her nerve pills . . .

Gladys: I found them . . . so no one needs to worry.

Robert: *(Breaking the ice)* Well, you're here. Let's order.

(The four sit. The WAITER walks over and hands everyone a menu. Everyone looks over their menu.)

Gladys: So what's good here?

Gloria: They have great sandwiches.

Gus: *(Continuing to scan the menu)* I'll be the judge of that.

Robert: Their burgers are terrific . . . you can't go wrong with their burgers.

Gus: *(Suspicious)* Really . . .

Gladys: It all looks good.

Gloria: I think you'll enjoy your meal here.

Gus: *(Who has been looking out, as if watching something)* Not with them sitting there.

(Everyone looks around)

Robert: Who?

Gus: *(Pointing with his menu)* Right in front of us . . . just look at them.

▸ *Drama Cue: Physical Comedy*

Everyone loves physical comedy, but it can be tough to perform. When a script dictates specific blocking, rehearse it over and over again. Well-executed physical comedy should appear natural and effortless to your audience.

Gladys:	*(Snobbishly)* Oh, I see what you mean.
Gloria:	What? Do you know those people?
Gus:	No, I don't have to. Just look at them.
Robert:	All I see is four people at a table.
Gus:	If you want to know what's wrong with America, your answer is sitting right over there.
Gloria:	I don't get it . . .
Gladys:	Gus and I are pretty good judges of character just from looking at someone.
Gus:	And from what I see, there is nothing but evil and worldliness at that table.
Robert:	How can you tell?
Gus:	Well, for starters . . . just look at how long that guy's hair is!
Gloria:	Yeah?
Gus:	He's a rebellious renegade. An antiestablishment freak!
Robert:	Just because his hair is a little long?
Gladys:	And look at that woman's makeup! She is just asking for trouble with that lipstick and eye shadow . . . but that's probably what she wants—trouble.
Gloria:	I don't think her makeup looks that bad.
Gladys:	Don't be fooled. If her mascara could talk . . . we'd all be shocked.
Gus:	Is it my imagination, or is that a gold earring in the other guy's ear?
Robert:	Yeah, it looks like he has a small earring. So?
Gus:	That can only mean one thing . . . he's an ex-con.
Robert:	You don't know that.
Gus:	I'm telling you . . . that man's done time! I'm guessing assault with a deadly weapon.
Robert:	Come on . . .
Gladys:	And look at their feet—look what they're wearing.
Gloria:	*(Looking across, over the table)* Sandals?
Gladys:	Yep . . .
Gladys & Gus:	Tree huggers!
Gladys:	Those four would rather you and I starve to death than see a species of cricket go extinct.

▸ *Characterization:*
Gus & Gladys Moment

Gus is opinionated, stubborn, and cantankerous. Gladys is cranky, contentious, and ready to rumble at a drop of a hat. Try to strike the proper balance in portraying these traits. If you take the comedy bit too far, their negative behaviors may not be endearing or funny. But if you overemphasize the negative, your audience will grow uncomfortable.

Gus:	Aha! I knew they were a bunch of godless human beings.
Robert:	What now?
Gus:	A tattoo! That guy's got one! I knew he was out on parole.
Gloria:	I'm confused. What does a tattoo tell you?
Gladys:	*(Ignoring Gloria)* Can you make out what the tattoo says?
Gus:	It's hard for me to see. *(Contorts and leans over the table)* Got it!
Gladys:	What does it say?
Gus:	The one on his bicep . . . U-S-M-C.
Gladys:	How terrible!
Robert:	So the guy's been a Marine.
Gus:	Yea, that's what they want you to think . . . it's a conspiracy. I saw on a talk show that USMC actually means Underground Socialist Militia Comrades. I'm telling you, that guy's dangerous.
Gladys:	And you know if those people are piercing their ears, and getting tattoos, and wearing earth shoes, they're probably doing drugs and Coca-Cola and everything else!
Robert:	That's ridiculous. How can you two sit here and cast judgment on those people just by how they look?
Gus:	Listen, I call them as I see them. And those four people are the farthest thing from anything good and wholesome that you'll find on the face of this earth!
Robert:	Then why are they doing *that*?
	(All four look at the table)
Gladys:	Their heads are bowed and their eyes are closed.
Gloria:	It looks like they are saying grace over their meal.
Gus:	*(Slowly)* Maybe they've all nodded off to sleep at the same time.
Robert:	They're praying, Gus.
Gloria:	I guess you two were wrong about them.
	(Silence . . .)
Gus:	Well, this means only one thing.
Robert:	What's that?
Gus:	They think they are better than us!
Gladys:	That's right, they're holier-than-thou!
Gus:	I knew it when I first saw them . . . Bible thumpers. I can spot them anywhere.

▸ *Caution: Physical Confusion*

When good physical comedy becomes physical confusion, the audience stops laughing and becomes annoyed. Wild expressions of unbridled hilarity onstage will interfere with the message of your drama. Remember, well-intended actions support well-understood dialogue.

SOUND:	**MUSIC TRANSITION OUT OF SKETCH**
Gus:	Anyone who prays in public is a grandstanding religious fanatic!
Gladys:	They've probably been talking about us . . .
Gus:	What's there to talk about?
Robert:	Hey, can we just leave them alone and decide what we're eating?
	(Everyone looks at their menu. GUS is staring off to the far left)
Gloria:	Hmm, the chicken salad looks good.
Gladys:	Gus, what are you having . . . Gus, what are you looking at?
Gus:	Oh, look at the group of people that sat down over to the left . . .
	(Everyone looks)
Gladys & Gus:	*(Looking at each other in agreement)* Liberals!
	(ROBERT and GLORIA hide behind their menus)
LIGHTS:	**FADE TO BLACK**
	END

▶ *Characterization:*
Gus & Gladys Moment

There is nothing like contrast in characters to bring out the most in Gus & Gladys sketches. Supporting characters should be countertypes in these sketches—develop supporting characterizations that are Gus & Gladys's polar opposites.

LITTLE GREEN PEOPLE

with Gus and Gladys Glum

TOPIC
Jealousy

SYNOPSIS
Gus and Gladys Glum celebrate an anniversary at a fancy restaurant as result of winning a gift certificate at an aluminum siding convention. To their horror, their former neighbors are dining at the same restaurant. It doesn't take long to see that Gus and Gladys are green with envy at the other couple's successes. We get to see just how ugly jealousy can be when the two couples end up sitting side by side.

CHARACTERS

Maitre d' – restaurant host

Lance Garrison – former neighbor of the Glums; husband to Dottie

Dottie Garrison – former neighbor of the Glums; wife to Lance

Server – waiter or waitress

Gus Glum – opinionated; stubborn; impatient; husband to Gladys

Gladys Glum – harsh; severe, insecure, wife to Gus

SETS/PROPS
Sketch takes place in an upscale restaurant.
2 tables with tablecloths
4 chairs
4 menus
4 water goblets
2 small flower centerpieces
Large outdated-looking corsage
Gift certificate

LIGHTS:	**BLACKOUT** *(Actors move into place)*
SOUND:	**MUSICAL TRANSITION INTO SKETCH**
GRAPHIC:	**TITLE SLIDE—** *Little Green People*
LIGHTS:	**UP ON STAGE**

(We see an upscale restaurant. There are two tables side by side at center stage. LANCE and DOTTIE sit at one table. They are looking at their menus and speaking to the SERVER)

Server: Do you need a few more minutes to look over the menu?

Lance: Yes, but how about bringing us out some of your Tahitian Calamari as an appetizer?

Server: Coming right up.

Lance: *(Smiling)* Happy anniversary, honey.

Dottie: Happy anniversary, dear. Tonight is going to be just perfect.

Lance: Dinner at our favorite restaurant!

Dottie: Peaceful. Quiet. Just you and me.

(LANCE and DOTTIE smile at each other and go back to looking at their menus. At that moment, GUS and GLADYS GLUM enter. GUS looks very uncomfortable. As always, GLADYS seems a little frazzled. She wears a very large and outdated-looking flower corsage pinned to her jacket. The MAITRE D' crosses to them)

Maitre d': Welcome. Do you have a reservation?

Gus: Yes, we do. Glum. Gus and Gladys Glum. Sorry we're late, but Gladys forgot her Pepcid-AC, so we had stop by the drugstore and get her a few hundred!

Gladys: Believe me, you'll be glad we stopped!

Maitre d': Ah yes, the Glums. Reservation for two. Another couple celebrating an anniversary. Love must be in the air, huh?

(GUS and GLADYS look at each other in slight disgust)

Gus: No, but those fish sticks you're cooking sure smell good.

Maitre d': It's calamari.

Gladys: Well "calories" to you, too! Let's eat. We're starved.

Maitre d': Just a moment. *(Reviews the reservation list)*

Gus: *(Spotting the GARRISONS)* Gladys, don't look now, but look over there!

▸ *Drama Cue: Simplicity*

You don't have to overdress the stage with elaborate sets or large props to create a specific atmosphere. In fact, a totally bare stage can help your audience use their imaginations. Let the dialogue transport the audience to your desired location.

Gladys:	*(Slyly looking around)* It's the Garrisons! I haven't seen them since they moved out of our neighborhood six years ago.
Gus:	Let's get out of here.
Maitre d':	I can seat you now.
Gus:	We've changed our minds.
Gladys:	No we haven't. I didn't get all fixed up to go and eat over at Captain Peg Leg's Fish and More like our last three anniversaries!
Maitre d':	This way.
	(GUS and GLADYS follow the MAITRE D' over to the table, trying to conceal their faces as they walk by the Garrisons. The MAITRE D' gives them each a menu, which they hide behind. MAITRE D' exits)
Gus:	Did you see that? They didn't even say hello when we walked by!
Gladys:	Ever since Lance got that new job, moved Dot and the kids out of our neighborhood, bought that new car, and became even more successful than they already were, they are so . . .
Gus:	Better than us! Look, Lance has hair now! Lance didn't used to have hair! How did he get hair?
Gladys:	It probably came with those artificial fingernails she has on!
Gus:	I wouldn't want hair even if I could grow some!
Gladys:	I wouldn't spend the money on beautifully crafted and fashion-coordinated nails even if we had the money!
Lance:	*(During the last few lines of dialogue, LANCE has noticed GUS and GLADYS)* Gus? Gladys?
Dottie:	*(Turning around)* The Glums! Gus and Gladys, what a surprise to see you here!
Gus:	Surprised? You don't think we can afford to eat at a restaurant like this?
Dottie:	I didn't mean that. It's just been so long since we've seen you two.
Gladys:	Six years, three months, twelve days and six hours . . . but who's counting?
Lance:	Our old neighbors! What a kick!
Gus:	Old neighbors? You'd look old, too, if you hadn't planted all that hair!

▶ *Characterization:*
Gus & Gladys Moment

Comedy needs to go somewhere. If Gus and Gladys are at their peak at the beginning of the sketch, there is nowhere to go with them! Therefore, work on pacing them. Build the emotional and physical comedy of this situation.

Gladys:	Don't you two ever age? C'mon, get with the program!
Lance:	So what's the special occasion?
Gus:	Nothing special.
	(GLADYS kicks GUS under the table.)
	Our anniversary.
Dottie:	Ours too!
Lance:	Happy anniversary.
Gus:	Yeah.
Server:	Would you like to start out with an appetizer before I take the rest of your order?
	(GUS and GLADYS look at a menu . . .)
Gus:	Yeah. Uh . . . we'll start out with some of this . . . uh . . . es-car-gott!
Lance:	*(In an effort to help them correctly pronounce "escargot")* That's "es-car-*go*."
Gus:	I don't want it to go. We'll eat it here.
	(SERVER rolls his/her eyes . . . and exits.)
Dottie:	So are you still living at . . .
Gladys:	Yes we are, and proud of it! We even have pool now! A Doughboy!
Gus:	You probably have a built-in pool, right?
Lance:	*(Humbly)* Yeah, a pool and Jacuzzi.
Gladys:	We still don't have a Jacuzzi yet, do we, Gus?
Gus:	And we'd have one if I got a better job like Lance, right?
Gladys:	Right!
Gus:	Maybe someone else should get a job and help out!
Gladys:	Then how could I keep my figure and have pretty nails like little Miss Dottie here? She was always the favorite stay-at-home mom of the neighborhood. Making us other moms all look bad!
Dottie:	*(Trying to change the subject)* Speaking of kids, how are Gil and Gilda?
Gus:	Who?
Gilda:	*(Kicking Gus under the table)* Our kids, Gus!

▶ *Caution: Stage Clutter*

Steer clear of using amateur stage sets that distract from the content of your drama. Simple boxes, stools, benches, and platforms can become anything your audience's imaginations want them to be.

Gus:	Great. They call us at Christmas.
Lance:	Robert and Wendy are both away at law school. They seem to be having a great time!
Gilda:	Must be nice to be able to send your kids to lawyers' school. I wanted to do that, but no, Gus had to have the Doughboy!
Gus:	So Lance, what are you driving now days?
Lance:	An SUV.
	(Jealousy causes the GLUMS to cringe)
Gladys:	*(Through gritted teeth)* We still have our 1965 Impala! So Dottie, still got the beach house?
Dottie:	Yes. We're spending a month there this summer. You should visit.
Gus:	A month's vacation at the beach? Did you hear that, Gus?
Gus:	Yeah. Maybe you should have married Lance!
Gladys:	Then maybe I'd have a built-in swimming pool! And an SUV! Smart kids! And a summer beach house!
Gus:	And don't forget nice hair and nails!
Lance:	I see you two haven't changed.
Gus:	What do you mean?
Lance:	Still the green little people we remember!
Gladys:	Green? I'll have you know I am an American!
Lance:	I mean, you two are still full of jealousy!
Dottie:	You were jealous of everybody and everything in the neighborhood!
Gus:	Us, jealous? *(Standing)* You think I want your marriage? Your hair? Your SUV? Your job? Your house? Your kids? Your beach house?
	(Starts to act as if he is going to say "no," but then . . .) Let's go, Gladys!
Gladys:	But Gus . . .
Gus:	In 'es car, go!
Maitre d':	Leaving?
Gus:	Yes. Would you get our car? It is in the va-lett parking.

▶ *Characterization: Gus & Gladys Moment*

Gus & Gladys love to be victims . . . especially Gladys. So when one spouse is lost in self-pity, have the other stand back. The background spouse's reaction should come once the other has finished his pity party!

SOUND:	**MUSICAL TRANSITION OUT OF SKETCH**
Gladys:	*(Stands, reaches into her purse and takes out a gift certificate and hands it to DOTTIE)* You may as well use this, since we aren't. We're here because we won a free dinner for two at this place at the aluminum siding convention.
Gus:	C'mon, Gladys. We're going to Captain Peg Leg's!
Gladys:	Whatever you say, Gus. Whatever you say!
	(LANCE and DOTTIE don't know what to say as they watch the GLUMS leave. Look at each other helplessly.)
LIGHTS:	**FADE TO BLACK**
	END

HEART TROUBLE
with Gus and Gladys Glum

TOPIC
Having a pure heart before the Lord.

SYNOPSIS
As always, Gus and Gladys are a little confused when they see that the marquee of a neighborhood church reads, Heart Trouble? Have Your Heart Examined Today! Thinking that they are stopping by for a cardiac examination, they receive another type of heart checkup.

CHARACTERS

Deidre – Church volunteer

Hannah Beasley – 30s; wife of Cornelius

Cornelius Beasley – 30s; husband of Hannah

Gus Glum – 50s; cranky, grouchy; opinionated; stubborn

Gladys Glum – 50s; rough; abrasive; clumsy

Pastor Phil – 30s; pastor of church

SETS/PROPS
Sketch takes place in the lobby of a church: Table, chairs, "Welcome" or "Information" sign.

LIGHTS:	BLACKOUT *(Actors move into place)*
SOUND:	MUSICAL TRANSITION INTO SKETCH
GRAPHIC:	TITLE SLIDE— *Heart Trouble*
LIGHTS:	UP ON STAGE

▸ **Drama Cue:**
Focal Point

If a sketch has a specific focal point, such as a piece of furniture, a door, or a window, try making that the only set piece onstage. For example, if the family dinner table represents the lack of family time spent together, then don't clutter the stage with other pieces of furniture. Allow the audience to see the table for what it represents in the greater context of the drama.

(We see the lobby of a simple church. DEIDRE (pronounced Dee-druh) is welcoming two newcomers, HANNAH and CORNELUS BEASLEY, at the church's Welcome & Information Table.)

Deidre: We are so happy you're visiting us today. I know you will enjoy our church, and you will love our pastor!

Hannah: We're excited to be here.

Deidre: Our pastor is beginning a new series this morning. He's calling it Heart Trouble. He is going to challenge us to keep our hearts pure before the Lord.

Cornelius: Yes, we saw the sign out front.

Hannah: We heard he was a great preacher and we also heard your church was very friendly!

Cornelius: The last church we visited, the people were mean and abrasive.

Hannah: Yes, we like friendly places.

Deidre: Well then, you've come to the right place. Everyone here is friendly and pleasant!

(GUS and GLADYS GLUM loudly enter the church lobby. GUS is hurrying GLADYS along. Their chaotic appearance startles the others.)

Gus: Sorry we're late for church, but Gladys had to stop off at the International House of Pancakes for one of her Rootie-Tootie Fresh and Fruity Pancake Marathons.

Gladys: That's right, there's nothing like starting the week out at IHOP!

Deidre: Uh, welcome to our church. Are you visiting with us today?

Gus: Yes, I'm Gus Glum and this is my wife, Gladys. Say hello, Gladys!

Gladys: Hello.

Deidre: So is this your first time here?

Gladys: Why are you asking us so many questions? Are you the head nurse around here?

Deidre: Nurse?

Gus: *(Looking around)* Seems odd to have our examinations done at a church, but hey, the sign says its free—right, Gladys?

Gladys:	That's right! Bring on the treadmill! I've had my pancakes, and I'm ready to wow ya! Wow ya!
Gus:	*(TO HANNAH and CORNELIUS)* Look, I know you two young kids were here first, but Gladys and I could go at any minute . . . so if you don't mind . . .
	(GUS and GLADYS push their way to the front of the table . . . HANNAH and CORNELIUS don't know what to think . . .)
	We're here to see the doctor!
Deidre:	Doctor? I'm sorry, you must be confused.
Gladys:	Look, Twinkles, I'm sure you've been the head nurse around here for a *long, long* time, but cut the chitchat and let us see the doctor!
Hannah:	There are doctors on staff here?
Cornelius:	Wow!
Deidre:	We do not have doctors on staff at this church.
Cornelius:	But they said . . .
Gus:	So who's doing the free heart examinations?
Deidre:	I have no idea what you mean.
Gladys:	*(To GUS)* Honey, the poor lady is way over her head . . . *(To DEIDRE)* maybe you should take some of the tension out of that French twist of yours! Might relieve some pressure on your brain! *(To GUS)* And she's a nurse!
Gus:	Look, my wife and I drove by the church this morning and saw the marquee out front. You know, the sign that says, "Heart Trouble? Have Your Heart Examined Today!" So here we are for our free exam!
Gladys:	Do we need to change out of these clothes?
Gus:	I'm not wearing a gown . . . let's get that straight from the get-go!
Deidre:	That sign out front is referring to another kind of heart trouble!
Gus:	Look, I have palpitations just like the next guy! Don't let my amazing physique fool ya!
Gladys:	*(Acting it out)* And my heart sometimes skips a beat. Sometimes I'm skipping all over the place.
Gus:	So we want the examination that you advertised, and we want it now!
Hannah:	*(Nervously)* Cornelius, maybe we should get our free heart examination while we're here as well.
Deidre:	No, these folks are confusing you.
	(PASTOR enters . . .)

▶ *Characterization: Gus & Gladys Moment*

Stay in character! It is easy to forget your characterization when concentrating on dialogue and blocking. Also, remind your actors that a great deal is said through body language—even when they aren't reciting lines.

Pastor:	*(As he enters)* Is there a problem here?
Cornelius:	Are you the doctor?
Hannah:	We were here first!
Diedre:	Pastor, apparently there is some misunderstanding about the title of your message.
Pastor:	On heart trouble!
Gus:	So are you a pastor or a doctor?
Gladys:	Would someone please just give us a straight answer around here!
Hannah:	Oops, I think I felt my heart skip a beat!
Pastor:	What is going on?
Deidre:	The . . . Glums . . . saw our sign and think that we're doing heart examinations!
Gus:	I need to get the old ticker checked out, Doc!
Cornelius:	Wait! I think I hear my heart murmuring!
Pastor:	The sign does not refer to your physical heart. The heart we are talking about is the heart that God sees! He wants our hearts to be pure before Him.
Gus:	*(Motioning to himself)* But what about our bodies?
Pastor:	You see, man looks on the outside, but God looks on the inside, at the condition of your spiritual heart.
Gus:	Look, Doc, I've lived most of my adult life with Gladys. I'm used to ignoring what's on the outside and trying to love what's on the inside . . .
Gladys:	You better watch it!
	(GUS and GLADYS stare each other down . . .)
Pastor:	Folks, this morning we are going to talk about the heart that God sees. He wants us to be pure. And through my message this morning, we will allow God to examine our hearts.
SOUND:	**MUSICAL TRANSITION OUT OF SKETCH**
	Well, I have to get ready to preach. Nice to have you with us today.
	(PASTOR exits . . .)
Hannah:	So where did the doctor go?
Cornelius:	He must have a medical emergency.
Gus:	He's not a doctor!

▸ *Caution: Anger Management*

When a script contains confrontational dialogue, be sure to bridle the intensity of the actors' emotions. Over-the-top anger and volatility performed on your church platform could backfire on you. Confrontations should be believable without being brutal.

Gladys:	Where did these two come from anyway?! Good night!
Deidre:	*(Trying to recover)* So will you two lovely couples be joining us for church this morning?
	(GUS and GLADYS look at each other for a moment . . .)
Gus:	You throw in an electrocardiogram and we'll stay.
	(DEIDRE winces . . .)
	We're out of here. You up for another short stack, Gladys?
Gladys:	Whatever you say, Gus. Whatever you say!
	(GUS and GLADYS begin to exit . . .)
Hannah:	So you're not seeing the doctor?
Gus, Gladys & Deidre:	There is no doctor!
	(GUS and GLADYS exit . . .)
Hannah:	Just like those other churches!
Cornelius:	Unfriendly!
	MUSIC SWELLS
	(HANNAH and CORNELIUS turn and exit. DIEDRE is exasperated and sinks into a chair . . .)
LIGHTS:	**FADE TO BLACK**
	END

▶ *Characterization: Gus & Gladys Moment*

Gus and Gladys need energy. Don't depend on costumes to carry the roles. You have to fill that costume with the kind of person who would put on those clothes! So remember: character first, costume second!

GREAT EXPECTATIONS

with Gus & Gladys Glum

TOPIC
Tithing/Stewardship

SYNOPSIS
A few interested visitors attend a church's New Members class. It is in this class where Gus & Gladys Glum prove that their expectation of church is to get and not to give. When the subject of tithing and Christian stewardship comes up, Gus & Gladys voice their objections and demonstrate their selfishness.

CHARACTERS

Wally – New Members class facilitator

Kendra – new Christian, wife of Jared

Jared – new Christian, husband to Kendra

Coral – looking for a church home

Gus Glum – opinionated; stubborn; impatient; husband to Gladys

Gladys Glum – harsh; severe, insecure; wife to Gus

SETS/PROPS
Sketch takes place in a church meeting room or Sunday school class: chairs, table, etc. Props needed: Nametags, church promotional piece

LIGHTS:	**BLACKOUT** *(Actors move into place)*
SOUND:	**MUSIC TRANSITION INTO SKETCH**
GRAPHIC:	**TITLE SLIDE—** *Great Expectations*
LIGHTS:	**UP ON STAGE**

(WALLY, KENDRA, JARED, and CORAL are mingling about in a church meeting room. Each person wears a nametag. After a moment, WALLY begins . . .)

Wally: I guess we can get started. Would you please take a seat?

(The group settles in to the chairs arranged in a semicircle.)

Sorry to begin a few minutes behind schedule, but there are two more people who had signed up to attend this meeting and I was waiting for them to arrive. But it looks like they are going to be a no-show, so let's start without them.

(GUS and GLADYS enter . . .)

Gus: Sorry we're late, but Gladys can't seem to read a map, and we ended up on the other side of town!

Gladys: I know how to read a map, but Gus doesn't know how to listen. I said left, right?

Gus: Right?

Gladys: Left, right?

Gus: Right you said left, or turn right?

Gladys: *(To the others)* You see what I put up with? Day in, day out. Over and over, incessantly . . . continually . . .

Gus: Watch it!

Gladys: You watch it!

Gus: No, you watch it!

Wally: Well, at least you're here. You must be the Glums.

Gus: Yes. I'm Gus Glum and this is my wife, Gladys. Say hello, Gladys.

Gladys: Hello.

Wally: *(Walking over and putting nametags on Gus & Gladys as he speaks)* Glad you arrived safely. And welcome to the "Getting to Know Us" church orientation class. My name is Wally, and I've been a member here at First Church for the past twenty years.

(GUS and GLADYS sit down.)

You're here today because all of you are interested in making First Church your home. I want to tell you about our church and answer any questions you have, but before I do, why don't you tell me a little bit about yourselves?

▸ *Drama Cue:*
Everyday People

Good drama speaks to ordinary people about everyday events—it doesn't have to be comedic or tragic in order to be effective. Create a "slice of life" with your drama sketches that people can connect to.

Jared:	Hello, my name is Jared, and this is my wife, Kendra. We just accepted Christ a few weeks ago . . .
Kendra:	And we were told that we need to join a local church and get involved.
Jared:	So Kendra and I are considering this church . . .
Kendra:	And wanted to know more about becoming members of First Church.
Wally:	Welcome to the family of God, and so glad you're here today. Next?
Coral:	My name is Coral. My family and I have just moved to town. My husband is away on business, so I am looking for a good church home for us. That's why I'm here today.
Wally:	Glad to have you as well. The Glums?
Gus:	We came to this here class because we're looking for a good church!
Gladys:	That's right! It's about time we found a good church! They're hard to find, you know.
Wally:	And have you been attending church?
Gus:	Yes, until recently.
Wally:	What happened?
Gus:	They asked us to leave.
Gladys:	We didn't see eye-to-eye on a few matters, and we spoke up!
Gus:	That's the fourth church we've been tossed out of in the last three years.
Jared:	You can get tossed out of church?
Gus:	You betcha!
Kendra:	Really?
Gladys:	That's right! Better mind your p's and q's!
Gus:	One slipup and you're tossed out like Gladys's cooking!
	(JARED and KENDRA look concerned.)
Wally:	Well, First Church is a kind and loving body of believers.
Gladys:	Yeah, we'll see.
Wally:	Okay, each of you has been given a list of all the ministries in our church. Do you have questions about any of them?
Coral:	How active is the women's ministry?
Wally:	Very active.

▸ *Caution: Normalcy*

When a comedy takes a serious turn, be sure your actors practice transitioning smoothly. You already know how the sketch starts and how it will end; work at making the journey believable so that the audience can experience the story along with the characters.

Jared:	And the young couples ministry?
Wally:	The best in town.
Coral:	Ben and I have five children. How strong is the Sunday school program here?
Wally:	Very strong.
Gladys:	How about the music program? Choir any good?
Wally:	Yes.
Gladys:	I sing, you know. I'm even good for a solo now and then!
Gus:	Gladys, that's why we were asked to leave church number one! You sang . . . and we were escorted out of the building.
Gladys:	It wasn't me. The organist started out in the wrong key!
Wally:	We have a great music program, and I am sure they would love to have you join them.
Gus:	Do you have any potlucks? I'm always up for a good potluck!
Wally:	Yes—in fact, we have one this Sunday night after church!
Gladys:	We were kicked out of a potluck at church number two! Gus and I got into a big fight.
Coral:	A fight at a potluck?
Gladys:	Gus decided to put yellow caution tape around my tuna casserole and I got angry!
Gus:	Gladys could have wiped out a whole generation of church members with one covered dish!
Gladys:	Everyone said they loved my casserole.
Gus:	That church was full of liars.
Wally:	Let's move on. You'll notice we have a full list of activities at Christmas and Easter, a missions conference in the spring, and our annual tithing and stewardship banquet in January.
Gus:	Just a minute, are you one of those churches that collects an offering?
Wally:	Yes, we stress tithing and Christian stewardship.
Jared:	What's tithing?
Kendra:	And stewardship?
Gladys:	It's when they pass the platter around and you put money in it.
Coral:	The Bible says that we are to bring our tithes and offerings into the church.
Gladys:	Something like 80 percent!

Coral:	No, just 10 percent.
Gladys:	You read your Bible, I'll read mine.
Wally:	As a church, we strongly emphasize tithing. It's how the work of the Lord is accomplished.
Gus:	I knew it, I just knew it! Another church that passes the plate! For once I would like to find a church that doesn't take an offering!
Wally:	Then it wouldn't be a church. God's plan for stewardship is very clear.
Coral:	And we should give cheerfully!
Gladys:	Like I said, you read your Bible, I'll read mine.
Gus:	We openly protested tithing in the third church we attended! We made signs, wore black armbands, and hired a ventriloquist to badger people when they entered the sanctuary.
Gladys:	That's the reason we were asked to leave church number three!
Jared:	We've only been Christians for a short time, but the way I see it, God has given so much to us, it's only right to give a portion of what we make back to Him.
Kendra:	I don't have a problem with that.
Coral:	And how could we have a choir, women's ministry, children's ministry, and so forth if we didn't have a way to fund it?
Jared:	Not to mention sending out missionaries.
Kendra:	Or reach the community for Christ.
Wally:	See, Gus and Gladys, there are a few people who understand the importance and mission of tithing.
Gus:	Well, Gladys, I told you! This church is just like all the others.
Gladys:	Frankly, we expected more out of this church! A little more ministry and a lot less emphasis on the pocketbook.
Wally:	But that's my point. How can you expect more from your church when you are not willing to do your part?
	(GLADYS and GUS look at each other for a moment. Simultaneously they tear off their nametags, then stand . . .)
Gus:	Excuse us, but we'll be on our way.
Gladys:	Call us when you've got more to offer us and less to ask of us.
Gus:	In the meantime . . . we'll continue our search for the perfect church! 'Bye.
	(GUS and GLADYS begin to leave . . .)

▸ *Characterization: Gus & Gladys Moment*

Gus & Gladys Moment: Good comedy can often be lost in the moment of fun. Focus on the details of a scene and don't get lost in the experience of comedy. Though this sketch will appear to be totally off the cuff, you must stick with your script and direction. I call this "planned spontaneity."

Wally:	Wait. You told us why you were asked to leave three out of the last four churches you attended. Why were you asked to leave number four? Was it because of tithing? Christian stewardship? Service?
	(GUS and GLADYS give each other another look.)
SOUND:	**MUSICAL TRANSITION OUT OF SKETCH**
Gus:	No, it was the coffee!
Gladys:	And the dougnuts!
Gus & Gladys:	*(To the audience . . . almost as if they are describing themselves)* Stale and bitter.
Gus:	Is it too much to expect the Sunday morning coffee to be fresh? Let's get out of here, Gladys!
Gladys:	Whatever you say, Gus! Whatever you say!
	MUSIC SWELLS
	(GUS and GLADYS exit as WALLY walks over and talks to the stunned newcomers.)
LIGHTS:	**FADE TO BLACK**
	END

▶ *Characterization: Gus & Gladys Moment*

Share the stage. Gus and Gladys are truly the stars of these sketches, but the other characters are vital for the storyline and message. Don't let the outrageous distract from the profound.

YOUR PRIORITIES HAVE SPOKEN

with Gus & Gladys Glum

TOPIC
Stewardship: Investing for eternity

SYNOPSIS
Gus and Gladys Glum attend an investment seminar hoping to strike it rich. Once they arrive, they realize that the seminar is presenting a challenge to make an investment in eternal things. With their finances in complete disarray, the Glums decide that financial discipline is too big a sacrifice to worry about.

CHARACTERS
Randall – financial consultant and seminar speaker

Gus Glum – opinionated; stubborn; impatient; husband to Gladys

Gladys Glum – harsh; severe, insecure; wife to Gus

Wilma Childers – wealthy

Bernadette – newlywed; wife to Bernie

Bernie – newlywed; husband to Bernadette

Persons 1 to 3 – seminar attendees (nonspeaking roles)

SETS/PROPS
Scene takes place in a conference-style setting. Rows of chairs face forward. Randall carries speaking notes; seminar attendees carry similar folders.

LIGHTS:	**BLACKOUT** *(Actors move into place)*
SOUND:	**MUSICAL TRANSITION INTO SKETCH**
GRAPHIC:	**TITLE SLIDE—** *Your Priorities Have Spoken*
LIGHTS:	**UP ON STAGE**

(RANDALL stands in front of a group of people who are awaiting him to begin his investment seminar. RANDALL looks as if he wants to get started. He is counting heads and looking at his watch. The seminar attendees are seated, looking through their folders or chatting to those around them.)

Randall: Well, we are waiting for one last couple to arrive. If they don't get here momentarily we'll start without them.

(GUS and GLADYS enter ... late and frazzled as usual. They are complaining to each other as they enter the room. Once they reach the front row ...)

Gus: Sorry we're late, but Gladys insisted that we stop to get her some sort of kachina-frapachahooey at the coffee shop down the street!

Gladys: A hot cup of frappé-cappuccino calms my nerves.

Gus: Anytime Gladys knows we're going to be talking about money, she goes berserk!

Gladys: And you all better watch out because I didn't get to finish that cappuccino, thanks to my caring husband here.

Gus: The coffee was stinking up the car!

Gladys: *(Turning to the group)* Have you ever tried to drink a cup of coffee while hanging out the window of a car racing 75 miles an hour down the freeway?

(GUS and GLADYS start in on each other when RANDALL interrupts them.)

Randall: You must be the Glums.

Gus: That's right. Gus and Gladys Glum.

Randall: If you'll take a seat, we'll begin.

(The rest of the group doesn't know what to think of Gus and Gladys. WILMA gives GLADYS the cold stare as GLADYS and GUS sit down next to her.)

Thank you all for coming to the Investing for Eternity Financial Planning Seminar. I believe each of you will leave today knowing exactly what your financial priorities should be.

Gus: We already know what our financial priority is! We want to be rich!

▶ *Drama Cue: Primary Character*

When a sketch is centered around one Primary Character (PC), other actors should understand that their roles are to support and not steal the focus from the PC. You don't want a battle for the spotlight here. Let your PC's character purposefully outshine the others.

Gladys:	Amen! Preach it, honey!
Gus!	Yeah!
	(WILMA is not amused. GLADYS and GUS feel the stares from the others. The room grows very silent.)
Randall:	Like I was saying, today's workshop is all about financial priorities. It's a proven fact that you spend your money on what you feel is important!
Wilma:	You're saying that how we spend our money is a reflection of our priorities?
Gladys:	*(Sarcastic)* Now this one here, she's a quick study! Quick study, I tell ya!
Gus:	Sharp as a tack!
Wilma:	Excuse me, but I paid good money for this workshop and I'm going to get every penny's worth.
Gladys:	Maybe you should have spent a few pennies on a breath mint! *(Waves her hand in front of her nose and turns to GUS)* It's enough to peel the paint off the walls!
	(WILMA reacts. RANDALL jumps in . . .)
Randall:	Shall we proceed? Now, in preparation for today's workshop, each of you sent in your last three registers from your checking accounts. We've reviewed your spending habits, and I think you will be surprised to find out what your financial priorities are. Anyone want to guess how you did?
	(WILMA raises her hand.)
	Wilma?
Wilma:	I hope my spending reflects my desire to spread my wealth to those who are in need.
	(WILMA finishes her line while turning toward GLADYS.)
Gladys:	*(Squinting like her eyes are burning and again waving her hand in front of her nose)* You're spreading something, lady!
Randall:	Someone else?
Bernadette:	*(Standing; is overly excited and in love)* Bernie and I are newlyweds.
	(BERNIE stands too)
	Our goal is to invest for eternity!
Bernie:	*(Hopeless romantic)* We want to invest in eternal things, not just temporal things.
Bernadette:	And we hope that our spending reflects those goals.

▸ *Characterization: Gus & Gladys Moment*

In these sketches, there is always someone who bugs Gus and Gladys and someone bugged *by* Gus and Gladys. This tension should be felt from the group from one particular character in each sketch. Be sure to block that antagonistic character close to Gus & Gladys so creative comedic interactions can take place.

Gus:	*(To Randall)* Can we vote people off the island? Because if we can, I'm voting these two off first!
Wilma:	How mean!
Gladys:	And you're the next one that's going, woman!
Gus:	The Glums have spoken!
	(BERNIE and BERNADETTE sit down.)
Randall:	Gus. Gladys. Why don't you tell us what your financial priorities are?
Gus:	We told you! We want to be rich!
Randall:	So where are you investing your treasure?
Gus:	Treasure? Who do I look like, Black Bart the Pirate or something?
Gladys:	Yeah, and I'm his talking parrot?
	(WILMA turns as if to comment . . . GLADYS gives WILMA the evil eye and points at her as if to warn her she had better not say anything . . .)
Randall:	Your money. Are you only spending your money on things that are temporal, or are you investing for eternity as well?
Gladys:	We give to the church, sometimes. Put money in the plate, sometimes.
Gus:	We sent you proof of that in the mail.
Randall:	I did receive your checkbook registers. *(Looking through his papers)* Yes, right here. Which of you writes the checks?
Gus:	I do!
Gladys:	I do!
Randall:	Okay. And which of you balances the checkbook each month?
Gus & Gladys:	*(Simultaneously)* He/she does! *(Pause)* You do! *(Pause)* I don't!
Randall:	So neither of you has any idea how much you spend or what you spend your money on?
	(GUS and GLADYS wilt . . . As RANDALL continues to read, GUS and GLADYS mumble excuses under their breath.)
	In the last few three months you two have spent $120 on cable.
	$200 on cat food.
	$300 on dog food.
	$450 on something called the "Lot"? Have you purchased a piece of land?

▶ *Caution: Overacting*

Larger-than-life characters walk a fine line between amazing and annoying. Allow your PCs to develop their roles to the fullest, but keep them from overacting, over-emoting, and overwhelming the message of the sketch.

Gladys:	*(Embarrassed)* "Lot" stands for . . . the Lottery.
Gus:	*(A pathetic excuse)* You can't win if you don't play.
Randall:	$320 on cosmetics and makeup.
Gus:	That's ridiculous! Gladys doesn't wear cosmetics and makeup!
	(GLADYS turns and gives him the evil eye and as she does she takes a tube of lipstick from her purse and puts it on.)
Gus:	$320 and worth every penny!
Randall:	You spend an outrageous amount of money on entertainment, fast food, bowling, and Krispy Kreme doughnuts!
Gladys:	What? We don't even eat doughnuts! We never . . . *(Looks at GUS like she just found out a big secret.)*
Gus:	I was waiting for the right time to tell you, Gladys. Yes, I struggle with eating Krispy Kreme doughnuts! I'm so ashamed.
Randall:	Shall I go on?
Gus:	You're just telling us all the bad stuff. Why don't you tell us what we've given to the Lord in the past few months?
Gladys:	That's right! So these people will know our eternal investments!
	(RANDALL doesn't say the figure out loud. He just walks over and shows GUS and GLADYS the page he has been reading off of. GUS and GLADYS look a little ashamed.)
Gus:	Doesn't that beat all. I was sure we gave more to ministry than that.
Wilma:	*(Smugly)* Well, I guess now we know where your priorities lie.
Gladys:	*(To WILMA)* I hope one of your financial priorities is medical insurance, woman, 'cause you're going to need it!
Randall:	Wilma! Gladys! We're not here to badger one another. We are here to take a good look at our spending and set new financial priorities.
Gus:	But we thought we came here so you could tell us how we can be rich!
Randall:	That's what I have been telling you, Gus and Gladys.
Wilma:	And I thought I came here to listen to you, not them! So either they go, or I go!
	(BERNADETTE and BERNIE stand.)
Bernadette:	That's right! We're getting nowhere with them here.
Bernie:	We need to make a decision! Someone's got to go!

▸ *Characterization: Gus & Gladys Moment*

Keep it civil. If Gus & Gladys heckle another character, make it funny. A comedic jab delivered too harshly will derail your intended laugh into an uncomfortable silence.

SOUND:	**MUSICAL TRANSITION OUT OF SKETCH** *Theme song to "Survivor"*
	(Music begins very strongly. No one else in the group seems to hear the music except for GUS and GLADYS.)
	MUSIC SOFTENS UNDER DIALOGUE
Gus:	Wilma.
Gladys:	Wilma.
Wilma:	Gus & Gladys.
Bernadette:	Gus & Gladys.
Bernie:	Gus & Gladys.
	(GUS and GLADYS turn to the others. The rest of the class simultaneously points to GUS and GLADYS. GUS and GLADYS are paralyzed for a moment.)
Randall:	Gus and Gladys. The workshop has spoken.
	MUSIC SWELLS
	(GUS and GLADYS stand . . . and slowly . . . sheepishly . . . exit stage. The others handle the situation like on Survivor—by looking a little embarrassed after the decision is made.)
LIGHTS:	**FADE TO BLACK**
	END

Smile! You've Been
RACHEL AND ROGERED!

Always the center of attention, Rachel and Roger feel most comfortable in the spotlight. And why not? They're believers, know their Bible, live life by the rules, and look great. Why *shouldn't* life go their way?

Teetering on the fence between self-righteousness and entitlement, Rachel and Roger manage to control every situation life throws at them. It's their church, their Bible study, their time, their way!

But you have to love them because when they show up, so does the audience. Your viewers will no doubt recognize some of their own behaviors being acted out onstage by Rachel and Roger. From a Bible study gone bad to yelling at people in the church parking lot after a message on patience, this overly pious couple will have your congregation shaking their heads and saying, "It's funny . . . because it is so true!"

Here are a few Drama Cues to help you produce the sketches featuring Rachel & Roger:

Image

Conservative, neat, and tidy is how Rachel and Roger show up! It is important to them that they look like the perfect Christians they want so desperately want to be. They are friendly and warm, but look out—they can turn on a dime and become domineering, short, and pious.

Wardrobe

There are many ways to dress Rachel and Roger, but remember how important keeping up their appearance is to them. Therefore, you might try Ivy League, preppy type of dress.

Paul's Favorites

Rachel and Roger sure can dress up an issue and then tell it like it is. Your audience will definitely identify with this couple. The following are my favorite Rachel and Roger sketches and the *Life Scripts* and where they can be found:

A Small Group's Big Problem / *Life Scripts for the Church: Characters*
Honk If You Love Your Church / *Life Scripts for the Church: Characters*

Want some ideas about what Rachel and Roger might look like? Check out photos of the original holier-than-thou couple at www.pauljoiner.com and meet Rachel & Roger!

And now, Rachel and Roger!

"My Father's in Control"

with Roger & Rachel

TOPIC
The sovereignty of God; our heavenly Father is in complete control

SCRIPTURE
Daniel 4:35

SYNOPSIS
Roger and Rachel experience a frightening flight, but for some reason seem to be the only two worried about the impending disaster. The stewardess and other passengers remain cool and calm. They've flown with this pilot before, and they have complete confidence that they will arrive at their destination safely because they trust the one who is at the controls.

FOCUS
When life seems completely out of control, remember that God is sovereign and is in compete control of every area of your life.

SETS/PROPS
Stage is set to look like the cabin of an airliner. This can be done by placing a SL and SR row of two chairs facing the audience. The number of rows depends on the size of the cast. Behind the back two rows should be a divider to be used as the flight attendant's station. The aisle should be wide enough for the action that takes place there. Passengers can have props they bring on with them—for example, magazines, books, pillows, blankets. Two emergency oxygen masks are called for if stage capabilities are available. Offstage microphone is required for the CAPTAIN's voice.

SOUND EFFECTS
Interior of plane in flight, Flight attendant request bell, Thunderstorm, Plane diving, Plane engine sputtering, Plane landing

CHARACTERS
Roger Melton – 30s; fearful, nervous

Rachel Melton – 30s; accommodating, scatterbrained

Flight Attendant – 20s to 30s; calm and professional

Boy – Polite, energetic, happy

LIGHTING:	**BLACKOUT** (Actors move into place)
MUSIC:	**TRANSITION MUSIC INTO SKETCH**
SOUND:	**INTERIOR PLANE CABIN** *(This track continues throughout the duration of sketch.)*
CAPTAIN:	*(Line begins in blackout, over music . . .)* Ladies and gentlemen, service to Springfield . . .
LIGHTING:	**FOLLOW SPOT UP ON RACHEL AND ROGER** *(RACHEL and ROGER look a little frightened and frazzled as they sit together in the first row. ROGER has the emergency exit seat card and is reading it.)*
CAPTAIN:	. . . It looks like we are heading into a weather front and can expect a bit of turbulence from the storm. I hope you'll just sit back and relax; everything seems to be under control at this time.
LIGHTING:	**LIGHTS UP ON ENTIRE AIRPLANE CABIN**
FLIGHT ATTENDANT:	*(Speaking in a microphone at the back of the cabin)* Because of the storm, the captain has turned on the seat belt sign and we would ask you to stay in your seat if possible. I'll be around shortly for your in-flight snack.
RACHEL:	How are you doing, Roger?
ROGER:	Not very good. You know how I detest flying! Not only am I afraid of heights, closed-in spaces, and honey-glazed peanuts, but now we're flying right into a storm!
RACHEL:	I know, this has been one bumpy ride from the get-go.
ROGER:	This whole flight has been a disaster so far. First hitting that flock of geese during takeoff, then getting locked in the laboratory, and then having the in-flight entertainment turn out to be the movie *Alive*. And another thing: Did you notice that our flight number is 13 . . . Flight 13?
SOUND:	**TURBULENCE** *(Passengers move with the turbulence, but no one appears worried except ROGER and RACHEL)*
RACHEL:	Oh, no . . . here we go again! Hold on, honey . . . hold on!
ROGER:	I gotta get out of here . . . I need some air! I think my air nozzle is broken.
RACHEL:	*(As if she is trying to adjust the nozzles)* Is it not working? *(Trying to feel the airflow from the nozzle to her face.)* Mine's working . . . I'll call the attendant.
SOUND:	**FLIGHT ATTENDANT CALL BELL**

▶ *Drama Cue:*
Offstage Focus

Scripts often call for the cast to look out over the audience at an imaginary person, place, or thing in reference to dialogue or action. When this is the case, designate a particular spot in the back auditorium as THE SPOT—a specific point upon which to focus their attention.

| **FLIGHT ATTENDANT:** | Yes, how can I help you? |
| | |

FLIGHT ATTENDANT: Yes, how can I help you?

RACHEL: My husband's air nozzle seems to be malfunctioning. He's getting a little panicky about it.

FLIGHT ATTENDANT: *(Feeling the air flow herself)* Hmm . . . You're right. Do you want to move?

ROGER: No! I want to stay put.

SOUND: **TURBULENCE**

ROGER: Ma'am, what's going on?

FLIGHT ATTENDANT: Just a bit of turbulence. There is a storm in the Springfield area.

RACHEL: Just to be real honest with you, dear, we are a little concerned.

FLIGHT ATTENDANT: There's no need to be concerned. We are in good hands. Captain Richards is at the controls.

(Attendant exits)

ROGER: Now I'm starting to feel sick. Do you have any more of that Dramamine?

RACHEL: Sorry, but you took all of it when we went horseback riding yesterday.

ROGER: We should have ridden those horses all the way to Springfield; it would have been a lot safer. Well, if this bouncing around keeps up, I'm afraid I'm going to get very ill.

RACHEL: Maybe another passenger has some Dramamine. I'll check.

(RACHEL begins going down the aisles asking people)

Excuse me, would you happen to have any Dramamine? Motion sickness tablets? One of those patches you put behind your ears?

(As she talks, there is again some turbulence, and as she walks she tries to catch her balance by hanging onto people's heads, shoulders, falling on their laps, waking passengers up from their sleep. Having no luck, she reaches the back of the cabin . . .)

FLIGHT ATTENDANT: Ma'am you need to be in your seat.

RACHEL: I am desperately looking for some motion sickness medicine for my husband.

FLIGHT ATTENDANT: *(Reaches in pocket)* Here are a couple of tablets . . . and here's some water. Please be careful. We'll be landing in just a few minutes.

▸ *Characterization: Rachel & Roger Moment*

Rachel and Roger are very conservative. They are not risk takers, and they approach any new situation with caution. So when these two are thrust into an unfamiliar setting, they react like fish out of water.

RACHEL:	Thank you.
	(RACHEL makes her way back to her seat when turbulence causes her to spill most of her water on a passenger. She continues back to her seat with the little water she has left.)
RACHEL:	Here you go, Roger.
	(ROGER takes the tablets)
SOUND:	**STRONG THUNDER AND LIGHTNING**
LIGHTING:	**LIGHTS IN CABIN FLICKER OFF AND ON**
SOUND:	**TURBULENCE**
ROGER:	This is it! This is it! We're going down . . . I just know it!
RACHEL:	Remember, our seats can be used for floatation devices!
ROGER:	You're right, should we practice getting into the crash positions?
RACHEL:	Let's do.
	(Both get into crash positions, leaning forward in their seats with their heads between their knees.)
BOY:	*(Noticing RACHEL and ROGER)* Excuse me, did someone lose something? A contact?
	(RACHEL and ROGER, noticeably embarrassed because they are behaving so strangely . . . They stay in their positions but look up at the BOY.)
ROGER:	*(Looking for an excuse)* No, we were . . .
RACHEL:	We're, uh . . .
	(Both say their next line simultaneously.)
ROGER:	Sleeping . . .
RACHEL:	Stretching . . .
ROGER:	She was stretching . . . I was sleeping.
BOY:	You folks okay?
RACHEL:	Fine. Thank you.
SOUND:	**THUNDER AND LIGHTNING**
SOUND:	**TURBULENCE**
RACHEL:	*(Looking across ROGER out the window)* Honey, do you know anything about engines?
ROGER:	Why do you ask?
RACHEL:	Because the engine on the wing . . . the turbines are not moving.

▸ *Caution: SFX*

Sound effects (SFX) can really enhance the atmosphere of your presentation. However, a sketch that calls for sound effects (or ambience) throughout the production should be presented subtly or they will distract the audience. "Volume up" the SFX as you transition in and out of the sketch to transport the audience in and out of your desired location.

CAPTAIN:	Ladies and gentleman, sorry about the tremendous storm that is bouncing this little baby around. You might notice that we were struck by lightning a few seconds ago and consequently we've lost an engine. Not to worry . . . we'll be all right. Everything is under control. Please prepare for landing.
ROGER:	We've lost an engine in the midst of a thunderstorm and he says everything is under control? I'm getting out of here! *(Frantically getting up as if to leave.)* I want a parachute!
RACHEL:	Honey, are you crazy? Get ahold of yourself! People are staring.
ROGER:	I tell you Rachel, this is it! We'll never make it through this alive.
RACHEL:	But, honey, no one seems to be worried but us.
SOUND:	**TURBULENCE**
LIGHTING:	**TURBULENCE EFFECTS**
RACHEL:	*(They both a take a look around.)* No one seems a bit concerned.
ROGER:	You're right.
RACHEL:	And have you noticed this young man across the aisle from me? He's as cool as a cucumber. *(Turns to BOY)* Excuse me, young man?
BOY:	Yes, ma'am?
RACHEL:	My husband and I were noticing how calm you have been throughout this frightening flight. You don't seem to be the least bit concerned.
BOY:	No, ma'am, I'm not.
ROGER:	Aren't you afraid?
BOY:	No.
ROGER:	Aren't you worried the pilot doesn't know what he's doing?
BOY:	No. You see, I know the pilot. He's my father. And that's why I'm not the least bit afraid. These problems may seem insurmountable to you and me, but believe me, they are nothing to my dad. He's brought me through worse storms than this little bit of drizzle.
SOUND:	**TURBULENCE**
ROGER:	But what about the engine, the rain, the lightning . . .
RACHEL:	. . . the fear of losing your luggage?
BOY:	Not to worry . . . it's my father flying this plane, and he has everything under control.
FLIGHT ATTENDANT:	*(Holding microphone)* Ladies and gentlemen, prepare for landing.

RACHEL & ROGER:	*(Looking at each other)* Crash positions!
	(They both take the crash positions.)
SOUND:	**PLANE LANDING, SCREECH OF TIRES, COMING TO A STOP**
	(Passengers calmly prepare to disembark, but can't help but notice ROGER and RACHEL.)
BOY:	We're here. I told you my father would get us home safely.
	(ROGER and RACHEL look around . . .)
RACHEL:	Look, honey, he's right.
BOY:	That's my dad, the pilot!
FLIGHT ATTENDANT:	We've arrived in Springfield. We hope your flight wasn't too rough for you and that you'll fly with us again.
	(FLIGHT ATTENDANT moves on . . .)
LIGHTING:	**FOLLOW SPOT ON ROGER AND RACHEL AS OTHER LIGHTS SLOWLY BEGIN TO FADE.**
RACHEL:	Roger, how's your stomach? Still afraid?
ROGER:	Me? Of course not. I wasn't afraid, Rachel, I had faith in that boy's father. The pilot was in complete control.
RACHEL:	You know, honey, I was thinking the same thing.
	(ROGER and RACHEL put heads together, as . . .)
SOUND:	**MUSICAL TRANSITION OUT OF SKETCH**
LIGHTING:	**FADE TO BLACK**
	END

▶ *Characterization: Rachel & Roger Moment*

Rachel and Roger can't seem to sit still—nervous energy is the key to characterizing these two. Their fidgeting shouldn't be distracting, but this little quirk makes them interesting to watch.

A SMALL GROUP'S BIG PROBLEM

with Rachel and Roger

TOPIC
How NOT to lead a small-group Bible study.

SYNOPSIS
The leader of a small-group Bible study does everything wrong when it comes to leading his Bible study group. After breaking all the rules, he is confused when his small group turns into no group!

PROPS
Each member of the Bible study should have a three-ring binder and study book. Chairs can be arranged in a semicircle.

CHARACTERS
Bible study group:

Roger – Bible study leader

Rachel – Roger's wife

Frank – Participant

Bonnie – Participant

Gary – Participant

Lucinda – Participant

LIGHTS:	**BLACKOUT** *(Actors move onto stage)*
SOUND:	**MUSIC TRANSITION INTO SKETCH**
GRAPHIC:	**TITLE SLIDE—** *A Small Group's Big Problem*
LIGHTS:	**UP ON BIBLE STUDY GROUP**

(We see FRANK, BONNIE, GARY, and LUCINDA sitting around the living room. They appear to be bored and waiting for someone. Finally, ROGER and RACHEL come running in . . .)

Roger: *(Rushing in)* I know we're late! You won't believe my day!

Rachel: You should have been there!

Frank: Roger, where have you been? You're 45 minutes late!

Roger: Frank, you're always one to exaggerate. I'm only 42 minutes late. And hey, I said I was sorry!

Lucinda: We were just starting to worry about you two.

Roger: We got cornered by another couple from our church . . . I can't tell you their names, but their initials are C & Y J . . . Something-son. Anyway, we got into a long discussion on sins of the past . . . actually, it turned out good, because I shared with them all about Bonnie's sordid past.

Rachel: Yeah, compared to Bonnie's past, their past is nothing. That made them feel much better!

Bonnie: *(Shocked by the breach in confidentiality)* I thought what we said here was confidential!

(Everyone agrees)

Roger: Sorry . . . but I am the leader of this group, and I felt led to use your testimony.

Rachel: Don't worry, He didn't give them your name. He just gave your initials and mentioned that you were the one who sang the solo last Sunday!

Bonnie: Oh!

Gary: Okay, so could we please get started with our Bible study?

Roger: Sure, let's have our snack time! Who was supposed to bring the snacks tonight?

Lucinda: You and Rachel!

Rachel: Oh, was it our turn?

Frank: Let me guess, you didn't bring anything . . . *again.*

▸ *Drama Cue:*
Minimal Lighting

Lighting (or lack thereof) can really set a mood. To convey a sense of pending danger or peril, use less lighting. A dark stage filled with shadows cast across the set and the faces of your actors can help create a mysterious atmosphere.

Roger:	*(Thinking)* Well, from the looks of this group, it's probably a good thing we forgot the snacks, right?
Rachel:	*(The only one who responds)* Right!
Roger:	*(Opening notebook)* Okay, so no snacks. What's next? Oh yes— an ice breaker to encourage dialogue. I didn't have time to think up one, but I think this will do. *(Adopting a negative tone)* What did you think of Pastor's sermon this past Sunday morning? Huh?
	(Silence)
	C'mon. Nothing goes out of this room . . . feel free to disagree with what was said . . .
Gary:	I thought the sermon was great!
Lucinda:	Me too!
Bonnie:	Took three pages of notes!
Frank:	It really touched me.
Rachel:	*(Apprehensively)* I think I liked it, Roger . . .
Roger:	*(A little taken aback by the others' positive responses . . . pretending . . .)* Uh . . . I did too. It was a great sermon . . . if you like that kind of theology . . .
Frank:	Could we leave Pastor alone and get into our study?
Roger:	All right. Next we have prayer time! Let's catch up on prayer requests. Anyone got anything they'd like us to pray with them about? Remember, we love you! Everything you say here is confidential. Nothing goes out of this room.
Lucinda:	I wish you would continue to pray for my relationship with my mother. She is still very bitter . . .
Bonnie:	She's still giving you problems?
Lucinda:	Yes . . .
Gary:	And it is really affecting Lucinda's health.
Rachel:	Poor thing.
Roger:	Lucinda, can I give you a little bit of advice? Get over it! If we hear about your mom, the dragon woman, anymore, I think we'll all scream—or join another Bible study group! Please! *(Abrupt transition from brusque tone to syrupy love)* All right, who else wants to share? Remember, everything is confidential!
Frank:	I need a little prayer concerning my job . . . I might possibly be laid off.

▶ *Characterization:
Rachel & Roger Moment*

Rachel and Roger can be self-centered. This selfishness is not expressed in a rude manner, but subtly— in their interaction with others. Find those flashes of self-righteousness in the script, then allow this odd couple to lose themselves in those moments.

Roger:	Frank, how many times are you going to threaten us with that story?
Frank:	It could really happen this time.
Roger:	I'll tell you what . . . if it happens, then we'll pray about it. Okay? Until then, ix-nay that prayer request! Now, who else?
	(Silence)
	Don't be afraid. You're amongst friends, and we accept you just as you are.
Gary:	I'm still having those medical problems.
Bonnie:	That's right. What did you say was wrong?
Gary:	I'd rather not say. Roger's the only one that knows . . . so if you will just remember me for medical reasons . . .
Roger:	Oh, come on, don't be so private. Good night, Gary, we've all known someone with a bowel obstruction before!
Gary:	Roger!
Roger:	Don't be a prude . . . why, we all know about Bonnie's plastic surgery . . .
Rachel:	You had plastic surgery?
Roger:	Or about Frank's cruelly placed boils . . .
Gary:	You had boils?
Roger:	Lucinda's hair loss!
Bonnie:	Hair loss?
Roger:	Rachel's nasty foot fungus!
Rachel:	I never shared that with them, dear!
Frank:	*(Very frustrated)* Could we please get on with the Bible study?
Roger:	Frank . . . chill out! Just because you're the dogmatic one of the group . . .
Frank:	What are you talking about, the "dogmatic one"?
Roger:	We learned in our small group Bible study training how to label the different problem members of our group. Like you're the dogmatic one . . .
Frank:	What?
Roger:	And Bonnie there is the supersensitive/touchy one!

▸ *Caution: Deliver Yourself from Evil*

Church drama that depicts an aspect of "spiritual warfare" should be presented tastefully. All too often directors go right for the macabre, and in doing so convey a sense of oppression when the lights come up. Let the dialogue present the message, not frightening makeup, costumes, SFX, or music.

Rachel:	We learned we have to watch what we say around her!
Roger:	Then you have Gary, the superspiritual one . . . and Lucinda, the slow learner.
Lucinda:	Slow learner?
Rachel:	That's right.
Frank:	And who are you two in the group?
Roger:	Why, we're the group leaders, of course!
Frank:	*(Standing up)* Come on, Bonnie, let's go!
Rachel:	What's wrong?
Frank:	I didn't come here to be insulted, trivialized, and labeled as a problem person. I came here for Bible study and fellowship!
	(BONNIE and FRANK leave)
Roger:	I told you he was a problem member!
	(LUCINDA and GARY stand)
Gary:	We've had enough, too!
Roger:	C'mon, Gary, maybe when you're feeling a little more regular . . .
Lucinda:	I think it's time you leave our house!
	(RACHEL and ROGER sit for a moment in silence)
SOUND:	**MUSICAL TRANSITION OUT OF SKETCH**
Roger:	It seems like the superspiritual one and the slow learner want us to go.
	Rachel, how many does it take to make a group?
Rachel:	More than one.
Roger:	Honey, let's go home. You and I will be the perfect small group!
LIGHTS:	**FADE TO BLACK**
	END

▸ *Characterization: Rachel & Roger Moment*

Perhaps Rachel and Roger want to be more aggressive but find that it is simply not in them. Portray their underlying frustration with moments of bravado followed by quick retreat.

The Adventures of Roger and Rachel in

THE GREAT ESCAPE!

TOPIC
Stewardship/tithing

SYNOPSIS
The Meltons are at it again . . . everywhere they go, they cause a commotion. Stuck in the middle of a crowded church pew, they discover that the pastor is scheduled to preach on stewardship and tithing. They're panicked at the thought of sitting through a sermon about giving money and plot their escape. After a few failed attempts at excusing themselves from the service, a couple of new Christians help them see the joy in giving.

SETTING/PROPS
Three rows of chairs or pews are needed to represent the church's sanctuary. Pews face the audience; each row should be higher than the one in front so that every actor's face can be seen.

CHACTERS

Roger Melton – 30s; nervous, dramatically square, hypochondriac

Rachel Melton – 30s; nervous, dramatically square, larger than life

Mom Flap – Rachel's mother; dramatic, as square as her daughter

Dorcas Melton – Roger and Rachel's square daughter

Philemon Melton – Roger and Rachel's square son

Craig – New Christian

Sheila – New Christian

LIGHTS:	**BLACKOUT** *(Actors move into place)*
MUSIC:	**TRANSITION INTO SKETCH (ORGAN)**
GRAPHIC:	**SLIDE 1—** *The Adventures of Rachel and Roger in*
	SLIDE 2— *The Great Escape*
LIGHTS:	**UP ON CONGREGATION**

(We see three rows of church members. Every row is full except the middle row, where MA FLAP has saved four places next to her in the center of the row. The congregation appears to be listening to someone at the pulpit. An usher stands by the back row. RACHEL, ROGER, DORCAS, and PHILEMON enter . . .)

Roger: See . . . I knew it! We're late! Again!

Rachel: I'm sorry, Roger, I told you that we ran out of hair spray . . . it threw my whole morning into a spin!

Roger: Your hair looks fine.

Rachel: Spray starch!

Roger: You're amazing! Look . . . we'll never find a good spot to sit!

Rachel: Mother said she would save us seats! *(MA FLAP waves)* Oh, there she is!

 Over there . . . front and center.

Roger: Dorcas . . . Philemon . . . over there, next to your grandmother.

Rachel: Go on, children.

(The MELTONS cause a disturbance as they "excuse" themselves going down the row to reach MA FLAP.)

Ma Flap: What took you so long?

Rachel: A bad hair morning!

Roger: What did we miss so far?

Ma Flap: The song service. He's giving the announcements now.

Rachel: Well, I didn't have enough time to get the kids to Junior Church. I hope the sermon is something they will enjoy!

Roger: *(Taking his bulletin and scanning the inside cover)* It should tell us here what he's speaking on. *(Eyes pop open)* Oh no! Oh no!

Rachel: What is it? What is it? A sinus attack?

▶ *Drama Cue:*
Line Insurance

Oftentimes a sketch will call for papers, files, books, notebooks, etc., to be used as hand props for the actors. Lines hidden amongst the props can be very helpful for introducing a novice actor into a drama. Though the rule should be that your actors completely memorize their lines, this kind of sketch can give a first-time actor a little line insurance.

Roger:	No . . . worse. Guess what the pastor is preaching on today?
Rachel:	What . . . what?
Roger:	Stewardship!
Rachel:	You're kidding! Say it's not so!
Ma Flap:	*(Leaning over)* What's wrong . . . what's going on?
Rachel:	The pastor is preaching on stewardship. You know . . . the Big T!
Ma Flap:	Tithing!
Rachel:	I'm afraid so!
	(MA FLAP clutches her purse to her chest)
Roger:	*(Dramatically)* Honey, we should have known. It's like the flu—it comes around every year at this time. Sermons on why we should give our tithes and offerings to the church. We should have marked it on our calendar and stayed away from here.
	(Congregants around them begin saying, "Shhhhh . . . ")
Rachel:	Honey, you're talking loud . . . people are staring!
Roger:	We've got to get out of here! Escape! Make a run for it before he starts preaching about money!
Rachel:	Thanks to Mom, we're trapped in the middle of a row!
Ma Flap:	How was I to know!?
Rachel:	You're the sermon scout, Mother!
Roger:	We've got to leave!
Rachel:	We can't just get up and leave without an excuse.
Roger:	Right . . . I got it . . . we left the iron on!
Rachel:	We used that last time. How about we've surrendered to be missionaries and we need to leave right away.
Roger:	That won't work! I've got it . . . the kids. *(Leaning over to DORCAS)*
	Dorcas . . . look at me, honey. Do you feel okay?
Dorcas:	Yes.
Roger:	Are you sure? You look a little sick.
Dorcas:	I feel fine.
Rachel:	You look a little puny . . . *(Trying to lead her)* We need to take you home because you're sick . . .

▸ *Characterization: Rachel & Roger Moment*

In Rachel and Roger's minds, everyone else is the problem, not them. They suffer from extreme tunnel vision and can't relate to those who have different opinions. But their cover-up is faux kindness; don't make these two mean-spirited.

Dorcas:	I'm not sick . . .
Roger:	I need you to be sick . . .
Dorcas:	*(Indignant)* That would be a fib . . . and I'm not going to fib!
Rachel:	Dorcas . . .
	(DORCAS turns away)
Roger:	See? What good does it do to bring your children to Sunday school every week when they won't even obey their parents? What do they learn in those classes, anyway?
Rachel:	The pastor's going to begin his sermon anytime now! We've got to think fast!
Roger:	If we can move to the end of the row, we can get out easier. Follow my lead. *(Turns to the person to his left)* Excuse me, would you mind switching seats with me? I don't like this seat . . .
	(The person in the next chair nods and stands up. ROGER slides into his/her seat and starts off a chain reaction of RACHEL, DORCAS, PHILEMON, and MA FLAP quickly moving over a chair. The person now must walk down five chairs to find a place to sit. Then ROGER strikes again . . .)
	Pardon me, but could I switch seats with you? The air conditioning seems to be affecting my sinuses . . .
	(Again the person nods, and the very same commotion happens with the whole Melton gang sliding over seats.)
	(To Rachel) Almost there. Ready?
Rachel:	Ready. *(Grabs her leg)* Oh! Oh!
Roger:	What?
Rachel:	I've got a cramp! A cramp! I can't go any further. I'll never make it out of the sanctuary! Roger, take the kids and go on without me. Save yourselves!
Roger:	*(Panicked)* Is there a doctor in the house? Anyone have some Advil? A heating pad?
Rachel:	I'm okay! I'm okay . . . the pain is subsiding! *(Embarrassed . . . apologizing to the rows around her)* Sorry. Excuse us! I'm okay . . . thank you. Appreciate it! Thank you for your prayers.
Craig:	*(Leaning over to ROGER)* Is everything okay?
Roger:	Yes, thank you. We were only trying to get out of here before the pastor began preaching. You know what his topic is for today?
Sheila:	Yes. Stewardship.

▸ *Caution: Line Dependence*

Make it a rule that your actors memorize their lines. If actors know they can be prompted, hide lines on the set, or write them down on their hands, they will not take the task of memorizing seriously. Your actors should know that memorization is just as important as characterization. Line insurance should be used only with a new actor or in an emergency.

Craig:	We're kind of excited to hear what he has to say.
Rachel:	You know the bottom line is money and time, don't you?
Craig:	Sure we do. That's okay. We're so glad that we have a church like this to worship and fellowship at that we don't mind learning about our responsibilities.
Sheila:	We've only been Christians for a short time. We used to help support the Scouts and civic organizations; now our money and time is going to something even more worthwhile.
Craig:	We see our giving as eternal investments in the lives of others.
Sheila:	Is that why you folks have been playing musical chairs? I know what you're doing. You're trying to sit next to us newcomers to set a good example, aren't you?
Roger:	Well . . . uh . . .
Craig:	*(Talking to SHEILA)* Honey, we can probably learn a lot from this wonderful family.
Sheila:	Thank you.
Rachel:	We're just glad we can be an inspiration to you!
Roger:	Just doing our part to contribute to you spiritual growth and nurturing process.
	(CRAIG and SHEILA smile then turn their attention forward once again. ROGER and RACHEL look at each other and look forward. After a few beats . . .)
Dorcas:	Mom, Dad . . . I'm not feeling very well. I think I'm getting sick! You better take me out.
Roger:	Uh-oh! No!
Rachel:	No way, little missy! You need to hear today's message.
Dorcas:	I'm not kidding . . .
Roger:	Just sit back and breathe through your nose, and think of your favorite Bible character.
Rachel:	No, put your head in your lap. Watch your bangs, honey!
	(MA FLAP attends to DORCAS)
LIGHTS:	**STAGE LIGHTS BEGIN TO FADE**
	FOLLOW SPOTS FOCUS IN ON RACHEL AND ROGER
Roger:	This ought to be a great message!

▸ *Characterization: Rachel & Roger Moment*

Balance Rachel and Roger's outlandish behavior with supporting characters who find their antics annoying. This contrast in characterizations will make Rachel and Roger situations all the more hilarious.

Rachel: I'm looking forward to it. And to think we tried to escape!

You know, Rachel, stewardship is not so scary. Next time, you need to start working on your hair a little earlier, we need to sit a little closer, and then we can dig a little deeper to support the ministries of our church.

Rachel: You know, Roger, I was just thinking the same thing.

LIGHTS: **FADE TO BLACK**

END

The Adventures of Rachel and Roger In

RACHEL AND ROGER'S NEIGHBORHOOD

TOPIC
Missions: Being a missionary in your own neighborhood.

SYNOPSIS
Rachel and Roger Melton invite a visiting missionary couple over for a time of refreshment and present them with a care package of items they have been collecting for them. The Meltons entertain their missionary guests in their front yard, and it isn't long before Roger and Rachel confess that they have nothing to do with their *worldly* neighbors. Staying inside their fence, Rachel and Roger have never made an effort to be a witness in their own neighborhood. The missionaries challenge the Meltons to target the mission field right in their own backyard.

SETS/PROPS
Front yard of the Meltons'. I suggest trees, bushes, and flowers with a white picket fence. A mailbox needs to be at the side. Lawn furniture is needed to sit on. Hand mirrors, a care box, a piñata, a baseball bat, and a tray of food will also be required. Signs are needed to hang on the fence as per script.

CHARACTERS
Roger Melton – 30s; nerdish, nervous, dramatically square

Rachel Melton – 30s; nerdish, nervous, dramatically square

Jan Norton – missionary wife

Dave Norton – missionary husband

Lindy Norton – missionary daughter

Mom Flap – Rachel's mother; as square as her daughter

Dorcas Melton – Roger and Rachel's daughter—miniature of Rachel

Philemon Melton – Roger and Rachel's son—miniature of Roger

LIGHTS:	**BLACKOUT** *(Actors move into place)*
SOUND:	**MUSIC TRANSITION INTO SKETCH**
GRAPHIC:	**TITLE SLIDE—** *Rachel & Roger's Neighborhood*
LIGHTS:	**UP ON RACHEL AND ROGER'S HOME**

(We see the front yard of the Meltons' home. White picket fence, trees and shrubs, maybe a pink flamingo or two. A mailbox sits to one side. Garishly bright lawn furniture is scattered about. No Soliciting and Keep Out signs hang on the fence. RACHEL enters, carrying a tray of snacks and a pitcher of water . . . giving directions to ROGER.)

Rachel: *(Entering)* Honey, just set that box down right over here. You're such a dear.

Roger: What in the world do you have in this box?

Rachel: It's the care package of various sundry items that the kids and I put together: toothbrushes, tissues, crayons, deodorant, insect repellant, itch cream, and chocolate. We're sending it back to Mexico with the Nortons.

Roger: Oh what a great idea. A little missions project right here at home. Now, when are the Notions coming by?

Rachel: Anytime now.

(The NORTONS arrive . . . enter stage . . .)

Why, here they are now!

Dave: Hello!

Roger: *(Trying to be missionary-correct) Hola!* Come on in!

Dave: But the sign says, "Keep Out."

Rachel: That's only for our neighbors! Come on in. *Buenos dias!*

Roger: Welcome to our *(overly pronounced)* ha-see-end-a.

Rachel: Oh, very good, honey!

Jan: Thank you for inviting us over. It's so nice of you.

Dave: We can't stay too long, but wanted to drop by!

Roger: Well, as you may know, we took the whole family on a missions trip last year to South America! And it changed our lives. Outside of some embarrassing trouble I had with a nasty parasite, a great time was had by all!

Rachel: Since then we've become very missions minded, and we wanted to send a special package back with your family when you return to Mexico! *(Pointing to the box)* Filled with all sorts of whatnots for the family!

Jan: That's very thoughtful! You're too sweet.

(MOM FLAP enters, carrying a baseball bat)

▸ *Drama Cue: Ensemble Casts*

Ensemble sketches are a perfect way to demonstrate a variety of approaches to one idea or topic. You'll find that your audience reacts well to ensembles because everyone can find a character to relate to.

Rachel:	Oh, Mom . . . Mom, these are the Nortons—the missionary couple I was telling you about. Jan and Dave, this is my mother.
Mom Flap:	*(With bat in hand)* Welcome. We've been waiting for you!
Dave:	*(Directing comment to the bat)* You have?
Rachel:	The bat, Mom . . . put down the bat!
Mom Flap:	Oh, I didn't mean to scare you. I thought the kids and I would break a piñata together for a little recreation.
Roger:	Where are little Dorcas and Philemon?
Mom Flap:	Well they were right behind me . . .
	(DORCAS and PHILEMON enter. DORCAS carries a piñata.)
Roger:	Kids, this is the missionary family I told you about. This is our little Dorcas, and this is Philemon.
Jan:	And this is Lindy.
Mom Flap:	Lindy, would you care to join us as we smash this pretty piñata together?
	You could probably give us a few piñata pointers.
Lindy:	Sure.
Rachel:	Well, good . . . Mom, why don't you go in the backyard with the kids? Now, be careful!
Roger:	And Mom, don't let them talk to those rowdy neighbor kids next door!
Mom Flap:	Let's go.
	(Kids exit with MOM FLAP. Ad-lib as kids exit.)
Jan:	What a nice family you have.
Roger:	Well, we're not fancy folks, but we love the Lord.
	(JAN and DAVE go to the picket fence and look out)
Dave:	And what a great neighborhood you live in.
Jan:	Do you have nice neighbors?
	(RACHEL and ROGER are a little panicked)
Roger:	Sadly . . . we don't. Don't let this quaint little neighborhood fool you.
Rachel:	Look, the Pierces, they're looking this way. Everyone turn around . . . quick!
	(DAVE and JAN are unsure what's going on)

▸ *Caution: Hot Dogging*

Some actors have a tough time being part of an ensemble cast. There is a tendency for actors to want to give more than what the script calls for, hotdogging for attention through over-the-top characterization. Actors need to be taught that blending in with the crowd is sometimes the most effective way to get the message across to the audience.

Roger:	Don't look at them. They could catch your eye, and then you'd have to talk to them.
	(All backs are to audience, and as each speaks, turns and looks over shoulder)
Dave:	You're telling me you don't talk to your neighbors?
Roger:	Are you kidding? They're . . . they're . . . well, let's say we believe we have the only Christian-family-values family in the neighborhood. Sit down and we'll give you the inside scoop.
	(RACHEL and ROGER sit in lawn chairs that face away from the audience . . . DAVE and JAN awkwardly join them.)
Rachel:	Mirrors up!
	(Again, DAVE and JAN are a little unsure of what is going on, but follow RACHEL and ROGER's lead as they take hand mirrors and look back at audience over their heads.)
	We'll give you a quick neighborhood tour. Over there to the right, with avocado shutters and rain gutters, that's the Worldlies.
Jan:	That's their real name?
Rachel:	We don't know their real name; we just call them the Worldlies. They are constantly blaring their wild music, throwing parties that last into the wee hours of the night. We're pretty sure there is consumption of alcoholic beverages. And there's all sorts of riffraff tramping in and out of their house.
Roger:	Next door to them, the gravel rock driveway? The Religiously Incorrect.
Dave:	Who are they?
Roger:	They are the neighbors that decorate their house for Halloween! Put a life-size Santa on their roof during Christmas! And have an animated Easter Bunny that colors eggs on their lawn during Easter.
Rachel:	Can you imagine having to live next door to people like them?
Jan:	Well . . .
	(Continually moving from house to house via the backward look through the mirrors)
Rachel:	The Untidy Lawn People don't control their children.
Roger:	The Broken Front Door People curse at their dogs.
Rachel:	The Brick House People are members of an opposing political affiliation.
Roger:	And then there are the Pierces next door.

▶ *Characterization: Rachel & Roger Moment*

Everyone in the Melton family should look alike. Ma Flap and Dorcas Melton are older and younger versions of Rachel. Philemon Melton is a miniature of his dad, Roger.

Dave: Their last name is Pierce?

Roger: We don't know what their last name is; we call them the Pierces because their son has his ear pierced and the daughter has her nose pierced!

Rachel: Yes, we live smack-dab in the belly of the beast here on Normal Street.

Dave: *(STANDS AND TURNS AROUND)* I know what your neighborhood needs.

         (Others stand and join him)

Roger: What's that?

Dave: A couple of missionaries.

Roger: What a great idea! Did you hear that, Rachel? Missionary Dave and Jan are thinking about moving into the neighborhood?

Rachel: We'll start a Bible study!

Dave: No, we're not moving in. We belong in Mexico. I was talking about you two.

Roger: Us? Missionaries?

Jan: Yes. You said you thought you were the only Believers on the block. This is your mission field.

Rachel: But we never venture out past our fence.

Dave: And until you do, your neighbors may never hear about Jesus Christ.

Roger: But hey, we've been on short term missions trips . . . we're sending a care package along with you . . . that's missionary work, isn't it?

Dave: Missions start at home.

Jan: Next door. Across the street. Around the corner.

Rachel: But they're all so different!

Dave: Just as different as the natives we work with in Mexico.

Jan: Or the pagans that come to Christ in other parts of the world.

Dave: Hey, look at the time. We've got to go.

Jan: Thank you so much for the package.

Rachel: The joy is ours.

         (MOM FLAP enters with an ice pack on her head)

         Mom, what happened to you?

Roger: Did you get hit with the bat?

Mom Flap:	No. After the piñata broke I got caught in the candy crossfire and was trampled by the children.
Rachel:	Oh, Mother, I told you to be careful. Now be a dear and show the Nortons out, will you?
Mom Flap:	All right . . . but it's pretty dangerous out there. Stay close.
	(Couples ad-lib good-byes and thank-yous)
SOUND:	**MUSICAL TRANSITION OUT OF SKETCH**
Roger:	What lovely people missionary Dave and missionary Jan are!
Rachel:	They're wonderful! Amazing.
Roger:	Oh look, the Worldlies are looking this way.
Rachel:	What do you want to do?
Roger:	Let's be missionaries, dear.
	(Together they slowly smile then mechanically lift their hands and wave.)
Rachel:	Look, honey, Mrs. Worldly dropped her groceries. She's in shock from the fact that we're waving at them!
Roger:	I say let's take that first step and stand on the other side of the fence.
Rachel:	Are you sure . . . we're not going too fast?
Roger:	Let's do it.
	(They move slowly to the front of the fence. They are nervous.)
	There. Real live missionaries.
Rachel:	The Great Commission never felt so good. What do we do next?
Roger:	I don't have clue.
LIGHTS:	**STAGE SLOWLY DIMS TO BLACK . . . AS FOLLOW SPOT FOCUSES IN ON RACHEL AND ROGER.**
	You know, Rachel, I was thinking: Maybe next time we make up a care package to give to the missionaries, we should make one up for our neighbors too. Who needs Jesus more than the Worldlies or the Pierces . . . right here in our own backyard?
Rachel:	You know, Roger, I was just thinking the same thing!
	(Heads go together)
SPOTS:	**FADE TO BLACK**
	END

▸ *Characterization: Rachel & Roger Moment*

Rachel's mother, Ma Flap, is just along for the ride. Ma Flap is a softer version of he daughter, but just as self-centered.

HONK IF YOU LOVE YOUR CHURCH!

The continuing Adventures of Roger and Rachel

TOPIC

Church fundraising campaigns/stewardship/debt retirement

SYNOPSIS

Yet another adventure with Rachel and Roger, an odd couple with a pessimistic view on life. In this episode, they are with Rachel's mother sitting in their car in the church parking lot, trying to get home. As they inch their way through the crowded parking lot they begin to discuss the debt retirement campaign their church is having. Roger and Rachel aren't too excited about making another commitment, but it is quite clear that they take full advantage of the activities and facilities offered by the church. Across stage is a visiting family. As they wait in their car, they express the wonderful experience they had that day at church. They can't imagine what it would be like to attend this church and wonder if the congregation there really knew how much they have.

SETS/PROPS

Two areas of the stage should be set as if they are cars. This can be done by lining up two rows of three chairs on SR and SL. The drivers of the car can pantomime the steering wheel. Brochures of the stewardship campaign are needed and are referred to in the script. Rachel will need a Day-Planner with a calendar.

SFX

Parking lot noise
Traffic
Honking of car horns

CHARACTERS

Roger Melton – 30s to 40s; nerdish, nervous, dramatically square, hypochondriac

Rachel Melton – 30s to 40s; nerdish, nervous, dramatically square

Mom Flap – Rachel's mother, a nerdish as her daughter

Tom – 30s to 40s; church visitor

Diane – 30s to 40s; church visitor

Mom – Diane's mother, church visitor

LIGHTS:	**BLACKOUT** (*Actors move into place*)
MUSIC:	**TRANSITION INTO DRAMA**
SOUND:	**CARS/TRAFFIC/ENGINES IDLING**
LIGHTS:	**UP ON SL**

(ROGER and RACHEL are sitting in the front seat of the car. They have just come out of the morning worship service at church.)

Roger: Rachel, can you believe all of these cars!

Rachel: This parking situation has really gotten out of hand.

Roger: We're never going to make our reservation at Marie Calendar's if we can't get out of the church parking lot.

Rachel: Patience, dear! Oh look, Roger, the Johnsons are going to let us in.

(Nodding and waving) Thank you! Thank you! Go ahead, dear.

Roger: Thank you! How's your mother doing?

Rachel: Mom? How are you feeling?

(MOM FLAP has been bent over in the back seat with her head in her lap.)

(Up until this point the audience has not had a good look at her. She rises up, and it turns out she has the same hairdo as RACHEL.)

Mom Flap: Just a little car sick. This stop-and-go stuff is hard on me, you know.

Rachel: I know. Here's some of Roger's Dramamine.

Mom Flap: What has happened to this church? I remember the days when you never had to worry about a place to park and it didn't take you ten minutes to get out of the parking lot after the service.

Roger: Yeah. Where did all these people come from? Don't they know it's Sunday? Why aren't they at the beach somewhere?

Mom Flap: We were here first.

Rachel: Now, now. You heard what was said in service this morning: Our church has practically doubled in attendance over the last few years. Who could have predicted we would have such a growth spurt?

Roger: All right, since you brought up the service, are we ready to talk about it?

Mom Flap: *(Looking around)* Ready.

Rachel: Okay. Lock the doors.

▶ *Drama Cue:*
Genre Sketches

When a script is written in a particular genre (i.e., cop show, western, detective, historical, etc.), do your homework. Watch television shows and movies that depict the look and feel you want to reproduce, and then incorporate genre-specific elements into your sketch.

(They lock the doors)

Remember, keep a smile on your face . . . you never know who could be watching. Look pleasant. *(She waves to another car)*

Roger: Sunday school?

Rachel: That was good.

Roger: Music?

Mom Flap: Great.

Roger: Message?

Rachel: That's always good.

Roger: Okay . . . .what about that drama stuff?

All: Uh . . . uh.

Mom Flap: I'm still not used to that.

Roger: *(Soured)* And what about this new fundraising campaign?

Rachel: Honey please, be careful, other cars are watching.

Roger: Sorry. *(Plasters on a fake smile)* Didn't we just come through one of those a few years ago?

Rachel: *(Fake smile)* Yes, we did. But honey, you read the brochure. This place is booming. There are so many things that need to be taken care of. If we can get rid of our debt, we can do so much more.

Roger: I like things the way they are. Just give me these dynamic services and I'm happy.

Mom Flap: Right. Anyway, how much can it take to run AWANA, children's ministries, and all these youth programs? All you need is flannel graph and some stale punch and cookies.

Rachel: But dear, there are the support ministries, our missions programs, the home Bible study fellowships . . . all of these programs are important and minister to the needs of our people.

Roger: But that's just the way it is, Rachel. We get something good going, everyone wants to join in. We have Jesus . . . everybody wants Him too. We buy the pews . . . strangers sit in them!

Mom Flap We sacrifice and give to build a new building and everyone and their brother comes to take a look. Like these people in the car next to us . . . .

LIGHTS: **LIGHTS UP ON SR**

(We see the other carload of people.)

Mom Flap: Who are they?

▸ *Caution:*
Message First

Your message is your mission. Lights, sets, costumes, and all other production elements should be second to dialogue.

Rachel:	I don't know, but they are waving at us.
Roger:	They look like visitors!
Mom Flap:	They probably got to park in the special "visitor" parking area.
	(Rachel begins to wave . . .)
Roger:	Rachel! Don't wave . . . .it might encourage them to come back. It's like giving milk to a stray cat!
Rachel:	Roger. You should be ashamed of yourself! *(Waving)* Hello!
LIGHTS:	**DIM ON SL - ACTION CONTINUES ON SR**
Diane:	Look, they are waving at us! Hello!
Tom:	Hi! I don't know about you two, but I have had a wonderful time at this church today.
Diane:	I can't wait to tell the people back home. The service was so special. *(Pulling out her bulletin)* Did you see all the areas of ministry this church is involved with?
Mom:	Incredible. It seems there is something going on at this campus seven days a week, 24 hours a day! I can't remember when I have enjoyed church so much.
Tom:	It must take a lot of sacrifice to operate a ministry this size.
Diane:	That's why they are planning to take "A Bold Step Forward" and meet the challenges of their debt. *(Taking out Bold Step brochure)* I'm not surprised to know that the people of this congregation are being challenged to dedicate themselves to prayer and sacrificial giving.
Mom:	Well, I can see that up to this point God has abundantly blessed this congregation.
Tom:	I wonder if these people know how fortunate they are.
Diane:	What do you mean?
Tom:	I wonder if they know how few churches have ministries like theirs.
Diane:	I wonder if they know the work and dedication it takes to maintain a thriving ministry such as this.
Mom:	A work this size can create a lot of problems.
Tom:	Yeah, but those are the good type of problems to have. I'm sure these people don't mind giving a little extra or waiting a little longer in the parking lot.
Diane:	Honey, why don't you let those people in front of us?
Tom:	*(Honks horn)* Go ahead . . . .
LIGHTS:	**FULL ON SL**

▸ *Characterization: Rachel & Roger Moment*

When Rachel and Roger's family get together, they match from head to toe. Their hair, their clothes, their accessories— they're happy being themselves and don't care to change.

Roger:	*(Flaring up)* Hey, no one honks at me! *(Yelling)* I'm a charter member!
Rachel:	Roger, honey! He's just letting you go in front of him.
Roger:	Oh . . . *(Smiles)* God bless you!
LIGHTS:	**SR FADE TO BLACK**
	(Slight pause)
Mom Flap:	Oh . . . how I wish our church would be small again . . . not so busy! Those were the good ol' days.
Rachel:	Mother. These are the good old days. Now put your head in your lap and hush it. We'll be home soon.
MUSIC:	Transition music out of script
FOLLOW SPOT:	**CLOSE IN ON ROGER AND RACHEL**
LIGHTS:	**FADE TO BLACK**
Rachel:	You know, Roger, I love our church. This is where I want to raise our children. You know how much little Dorcas and Philemon get out of their church activities. I can't imagine going anywhere else.
Roger:	Maybe it's time to put the pedal to the medal and take that bold step forward.
Rachel:	You know, Roger, I was just thinking the same thing!
FOLLOW SPOT:	**FRAMES ROGER AND RACHEL'S FACES . . . CLOSE TO BLACK**
	END

▸ *Characterization: Rachel & Roger Moment*

There's nothing like patronizing people who are different from us . . . and Rachel and Roger are good at that. When they encounter unique individuals, they immediately expect the worst and label them with a stereotype. It's this characteristic that makes us like Rachel and Roger . . . they say what we want to but don't dare!

GOING NOWHERE FAST

The continuing adventures of Rachel and Roger

TOPIC

The importance of having corporate vision

SCRIPTURE

Proverbs 29:18 "Where there is no vision, the people perish . . . "

SYNOPSIS

The somewhat neurotic and obnoxious Roger and Rachel Melton are on yet another adventure turned bad. This time, on a backpacking excursion with fellow recreation club members, the couple finds themselves unprepared for the journey. It seems no one knows what direction they're heading, how or when they're getting there, what they'll eat, where they'll stay, or what they're going to do once they arrive. It is apparent that the recreation club has no vision, direction, or preparation for this adventure.

SET/PROPS

The set should suggest a mountain trail. Trees, rocks, and plants might lend to the atmosphere. Each of the backpackers should not be too well equipped, since they each believe someone else is going to take care of them.

CHARACTERS

Roger Melton – 30s to 40s: nervous, dramatic, square, hypochondriac

Rachel Melton – 30s to 40s: nervous, dramatic, square

Jenny – 20s to 30s: fussy, well-to-do, particular

Dorothy – 40s to 50s: serious, no-nonsense

Bernie – 40s to 50s: laid-back, easygoing

LIGHTS:	**BLACKOUT** *(Actors move into place)*
GRAPHIC:	**SLIDE 1—** *The Adventures of Roger and Rachel*
	SLIDE 2— *Today's Episode: Going Nowhere Fast*
SOUND:	**MUSICAL TRANSITION INTO SKETCH**
LIGHTS:	**LIGHTS UP – MOUNTAIN TRAIL**
SOUND:	**MOUNTAIN TRAIL ENVIRONMENT SFX**

(BERNIE, DOROTHY, and JENNY struggle up onstage. They appear to be tired and winded from hiking.)

Dorothy: Wait. Can't we stop and rest a minute? I gotta catch my breath.

Jenny: Yes. I second that motion! Besides, I think we lost Rachel and Roger at that last turn.

Bernie: *(Looking back and calling)* Rachel? Roger?

Roger: *(Offstage, then entering)* We're right behind you. C'mon, Rachel. Quit feeding the squirrels and keep moving.

Rachel: *(Throwing a cheese puff to an imaginary squirrel)* I've made so many cute little friends on this trail. There you go . . . look how they love those cheese puffs.

Dorothy: We thought we'd stop for a minute. We all needed a little breather.

Roger: Yes! Good idea. This hike is killing me! C'mon, Rachel, let's rest a minute.

(The group looks out at the wide expanse in front of them.)

Jenny: What a breathtaking view!

Dorothy: Spectacular!

Bernie: Beauty as far as the eye can see!

Roger: How majestic!

Rachel: I've always wanted to climb Mt. Shasta!

(The group looks puzzled.)

Roger: No, Rachel . . . we're not climbing Mt Shasta. We're climbing . . .

(Following names are spoken simultaneously . . .)

Roger: Mt. Ararat!

Bernie: Mt. McKinley!

▸ *Characterization: Rachel & Roger Moment*

"Perfect in every way"—that's how Rachel and Roger would describe themselves. Even in the worst situations they both look terrific. They may not have it all together on the inside, but you would never know it just by looking at them.

Dorothy:	Mt. Whitney!
Jenny:	Mt. Rushmore!
	(Everyone stops and looks at each other.)
Bernie:	We've been climbing Mt. McKinley!
Dorothy:	No, we're not. This mountain is Mt. Whitney!
Jenny:	Well, I was under the impression that we were hiking up Mt. Rushmore! No wonder I haven't seen a familiar face.
Roger:	You are all wrong! We are climbing Mt. Ararat.
All:	What?
Roger:	Aren't we on an ICR excursion looking for the Ark?
Rachel:	It's the altitude . . . Roger's a little confused.
Dorothy:	Then what mountain are we on?
	(Everyone stops and stares at each other.)
Roger:	Oh, this is great! I'm climbing some mountain, and I don't even know why.
Rachel:	Why are we climbing this mountain?
Roger:	You said you wanted to.
Rachel:	All I said is that sometime soon I would like to go to Magic Mountain.
Roger:	Well, there's nothing magic about this mountain!
Dorothy:	I thought we were looking for Bigfoot!
Bernie:	Bigfoot? I thought we were going to be the first expedition to climb to the top of Mt. McKinley!
Dorothy:	That was done a long time ago!
Bernie:	No kidding? *(To JENNY)* Why are you here?
Jenny:	I don't know. I just followed the crowd.
Roger:	Not only do we not know what mountain we are on, we have no idea why we are climbing it. I have a bad feeling about this! *(ROGER pulls out an asthma inhaler and takes a puff on it.)*
Rachel:	Now don't panic, Roger. Let's just keep calm. Maybe you should take some Dramamine. How about a little water?
Roger:	That would be good.
Rachel:	All right, who has the water?

▸ *Drama Cue:*
Prop Placement

If your drama centers around a specific prop, be sure that prop is identifiable, professional looking, and placed where it can easily be seen. Don't make your audience search to find the "star" of the show.

(Again, everyone stares at one another.)

Dorothy: Don't look at me. I wasn't in charge of water.

Bernie: I would have brought a canteen if someone had asked me to.

Jenny: I thought it was someone else's responsibility.

Roger: Rachel?

Rachel: I was in charge of the towelettes!

Roger: So we're stuck out here without any water!

Jenny: Maybe there will be some drinking fountains along the way.

(They all give JENNY "the look.")

Rachel: Okay . . . no one panic! Maybe what we should do is eat, then decide what course of action to take. It's hard to make decisions on an empty stomach.

Roger: Good idea, Rachel. Let's eat.

(Each member of the group prepares to eat. Roger and Rachel wipe their hands with the towelettes. Dorothy takes out a fork and spoon from her purse. Jenny takes out some money. Bernie tucks a napkin in his collar. They are all ready to eat. Nothing happens . . . they stare at each other.)

Bernie: So . . . let's eat.

Dorothy: Yes, I'm starved.

(Again they all stare at each other.)

Roger: Let me guess! No one brought the food! Who was in charge of bringing the food?

Rachel: Well, I didn't think we could bring any food into Magic Mountain . . . so I didn't bring any.

Dorothy: I heard the hike was being catered!

Bernie: I heard a rumor about a McDonalds at the top of trail 2.

Jenny: I thought food was someone else's responsibility!

Rachel: There's always berries, dear!

Bernie: I wonder how many berries would equal a Big Mac!

Roger: Everyone check in their bags for something we could eat . . . Rachel, you have cheese puffs!

Rachel: I fed them to the squirrels.

Dorothy: I have a crushed packet of Saltines.

▸ *Caution: Sound Advice*

An SFX-specific sketch needs special finessing by both the director and the sound engineer. Sound cues need to be discussed before rehearsal starts. Also, as with any technical cue, an SFX cue should be written into you script. One final tip: Your technical crew should always receive their scripts on the same day as the actors.

Bernie:	I found a stray peanut in the bottom of my pack.
Jenny:	I have spearmint-flavored dental floss!
Roger:	We're doomed! Who was in charge of this expedition, anyway?
	(Everyone in the group points to a different person.)
	Who was supposed to know our itinerary?
	(Again, everyone points to someone else.)
	Who thinks we are in big trouble?
	(They all raise their hands.)
Bernie:	What do we do? Go back?
Dorothy:	It's going to be dark soon!
Jenny:	What time do we have to check in?
	(Again, stares . . .)
Rachel:	Checked in where, honey?
Jenny:	Our hotel . . . the Hyatt.
Bernie:	We're staying in tents . . . aren't we? Did anyone bring the . . . forget it.
LIGHTS:	**LIGHTS ARE SLOWLY FADING FROM DAYLIGHT TO NIGHT**
SOUND:	**CROSSFADE INTO CRICKET AND OWL SOUNDS**
Roger:	Rachel . . . can I see you a moment?
	(ROGER and RACHEL move downstage.)
Rachel:	Yes dear, what is it?
Roger:	I can't believe all this! What were we thinking? If it gets bad, dear, it's you and me. We might have to go it alone!
Rachel:	What do you mean?
Roger:	It might get real ugly up here. When people have no direction, no leader, and no hope, they can get crazy . . . you know. We can use your pocketbook and my shoes for weapons to protect ourselves. Watch your back—you can't trust anyone out here in the wild. You know Bernie?
Rachel:	Yeah.
Roger:	He's holding out on us. I think I saw some Ding-Dongs in his bag. Keep an eye on him.
	(RACHEL and ROGER return.)

▶ *Characterization:*
Rachel & Roger Moment

Though Rachel and Roger are conservative, they are also very expressive. Many times these two wind up in some very funny physical comedy situations. Contrast their conservative appearance with their outrageous actions.

Dorothy:	Come up with a plan?
Roger:	Afraid not . . .
SFX:	**NIGHT CALL OF WOLVES**
Jenny:	What was that?
Bernie:	Sounds pretty close.
Rachel:	I wonder what they will think.
Roger:	What who will think?
Rachel:	I wonder what the rescue party will think when they find five lifeless hikers with spearmint floss hanging from their mouths.
LIGHTS:	**TO FULL NIGHT WASH – BRING UP SPOT ON RACHEL AND ROGER**
Roger:	Rachel, if we ever get back to civilization in one piece, I think it would be to our advantage to be a little more concerned where we are going and how we are going to get there . . . before we leave the house.
Rachel:	You know, Roger, I was just thinking the very same thing.
LIGHTS:	**FADE WASH TO BLACK . . . FADE SPOTLIGHT**
	END

Lights! Camera! Action!

IT'S BRIDGET & BRANDON!

Welcome to the set of *Home Grown*, co-hosted by Bridget and Brandon! From the moment you walk onto the set you'll realize that Bridget and Brandon don't know much, but they do know how to schmooze. That's their job—they're talk show hosts, after all. All they know to do is smile, laugh, chortle, and sensationalize the topic of the day.

Bridget and Brandon are always on. Because they have been working together for years, they play off one another very well; their banter is seamless.

Here are a few Drama Cues to help you produce the sketches featuring Bridget and Brandon:

Image

Bridget and Brandon are larger than life, dressed to the nines, perfectly groomed, and love their close-ups! You might even notice that these two drink coffee *at the same time*, look at the camera *at the same time*, laugh *at the same time,* and agree with their guests *at the same time*! They are mirror images of each other, and their actions and verbal cues prove it.

Wardrobe

For costumes, dress Bridget and Brandon in colorful business attire or flashy casual. Bling is big with these two, so go for the outrageous and the shiny.

Set

Create a *Home Grown* set with a table and chairs for interviews and a table off to the side for those sketches that include demonstrations. The focus of these sketches should be Bridget and Brandon, so make the set secondary—but reflective of the hosts' personalities.

Video & Audio

Don't be afraid to take a camera out and create a thirty-second show roll-in. Find some theme music and let the audience see Bridget and Brandon walking in the park, cooking, gardening, riding horses, or any other activity. And don't forget the close-ups with this video. For example, even if these two are just planting flowers, their focus is on how they look!

Tip: If you don't have the resources to create a video, use some great jazz as the show's theme song at the beginning and end of each sketch.

Paul's Favorites

Bridget and Brandon are very dramatic—I guess that's why I like to watch them perform. The following are my two favorite Bridget & Brandon sketches:

Home Grown / *Life Scripts: Characters*
Home Grown: This Is Your Tithe / *Life Scripts: Characters*

Want some ideas about what Bridget and Brandon might look like? Check out their headshots and promotional photos at www.pauljoiner.com and meet Bridget and Brandon!

Are you ready for Bridget and Brandon's close-up? Action!

HOME GROWN

with Bridget & Brandon

TOPIC

Spiritual growth due to home Bible study groups.

SYNOPSIS

The Home Grown Show with Bridget and Brandon is a morning talk show that features home improvement segments, gardening tips, and cooking demonstrations. Jack Gordon, author of *Community Planting*, is the special guest on today's show. Bridget and Brandon expect the interview to focus on beautifying a community by planting plants, flowers, trees, and shrubs. Our co-hosts are in for a surprise—they're about to learn that Jack means another type of community planting.

SETTING

Sketch takes place on a typical *Home Grown* set, decorated with flowers, books, plants, etc. A table or counter should be set up with gardening materials on it. Sketch can begin with a thirty- to sixty-second video/slide lead-in of Bridget and Brandon to give the audience a feel of watching the show on television or watching "live" in the studio.

CHARACTERS

BRIDGET – *Home Grown* co-host: exaggerated, dramatic, clueless

BRANDON – *Home Grown* co-host: conceited, finds himself charming and witty

ANNOUNCER – Introduces *The Home Grown Show* off-stage with microphone

JACK GORDON – Guest, author of the book *Community Planting*

SCOTT SMITH – Result of spiritual planting in a home Bible study group

LILY SMITH – Result of spiritual planting in a home Bible study group

LIGHTS:	**BLACKOUT** *(Actors move into place)*
GRAPHIC:	**OPENING MUSIC/VIDEO SEGMENT FOR** *The Home Grown Show*
	(If you have access to a video production crew, create a high-energy talk show opening sequence. The soundtrack should reflect a "talk show" feel. Show various poses of Bridget and Brandon around the set. Without video, create a slideshow of photos to develop the same effect.)
Announcer:	It's *Home Grown with Bridget and Brandon*!
	(MUSIC, and/or VIDEO/SLIDES continue)
	And here are your hosts, Bridget and Brandon!
LIGHTS:	**LIGHTS UP— SL:** *HOME GROWN* **SET**
	(BRIDGET and BRANDON enter overly decorated Home Grown television set. They are dramatic, pretentious, and sparkling with enthusiasm.)
Brandon:	Welcome to another edition of *The Home Grown Show*, the daily home information show. I'm Brandon . . .
Bridget:	. . . and I'm Bridget, and we have a wonderful show planned for you today.
Brandon:	Yesterday's show had us in the garage refinishing antique furniture and then in the kitchen whipping up tasty summer treats. Today, our efforts will be concentrated in the garden.
Bridget:	*(Trying to simulate spontaneity)* Do you have much of a green thumb, Brandon?
Brandon:	*(Trying for humor)* I don't know, but I've been told I'm "all thumbs!"
	(Laughs)
Bridget:	*(Laughing)* No, a *green* thumb, silly!
Brandon:	*(Cool)* Hey, what can I say! My Chia Pet didn't even grow!
Bridget:	*(Giggling)* Stop! I'm trying to do a show here!
Brandon:	Okay, okay! But, what can I say! I can't help being witty.
Bridget:	We all know what joy a garden brings us at home, but what about the beauty that trees, flowers, and shrubs give to our communities?
Brandon:	Our guest today is author of the book *(holding book up)* *Community Planting,* and we have invited him here today to help us learn how we can beautify our city. Help me welcome Jack Gordon.
SOUND:	*HOME GROWN* **THEME & APPLAUSE**

▸ *Drama Cue: Simple Connections*

To help make your drama memorable, try connecting your characters in some noticeable way. This can be done through costumes, makeup, hairstyle, or mannerisms. In this sketch, each women might wear a larger-than-life hat—different from each other, but similar in style. You'll find that your audience will recall them as "The Hat Ladies." (I see a sequel in the making . . .)

(JACK enters and is greeted by the hosts. They all sit.)

Brandon: Jack, welcome to the show. First, I must apologize for Bridget and myself. We haven't had time to look at your book, we just returned from co-anchoring the Barbie and Ken Springtime Parade.

Bridget: Oops! Sorry, Jack.

Brandon: But we're guessing that Community Planting is all about planting beauty in our towns.

Jack: That's right. Planting that brings a harvest of community spirit, belonging, care, and family.

Bridget: Family? Planting helps families?

Jack: Yes, and marriages.

Brandon: The family that gardens together . . . stays together?

Jack: Well, almost. I think you two are a little confused about the planting I am referring to. I'm not talking about potting plants and trees; I'm talking about the planting of group Bible studies in homes.

Brandon &
Bridget: *(Dazed and confused)* Oh.

Jack: Our church has found that planting home Bible studies has benefited individuals and families in our church community.

Brandon: *(Still trying to figure it out)* So when do you plant?

Jack: In the fall each year.

Bridget: And you plant seeds, sprouts, bulbs?

Brandon: No, Bridget. He's talking about people . . . church.

Jack: We plant people in the enriched soil of love, care, and belonging of other Christians.

Brandon: What have the results been? How have you done?

Jack: I'd like you to meet some of our blossoms. Scott, Lily, could you come out here, please?

SOUND: *HOME GROWN THEME SONG*

(LILY and SCOTT enter and join the others on stage)

Jack: Bridget and Brandon, I'd like you to meet Scott and Lily Smith. They have just completed their first year in a home Bible study group.

Bridget: *(Still not getting it)* This couple gardens too? And . . . you grew Lily in your garden? Are you a water lily? Tiger lily? Uh . . .

Brandon: No, Bridget.

▸ *Characterization:*
Bridget & Brandon
Moment

Bridget and Brandon are always ready for their close-ups. From time to time, have each of them hold their expression for the audience/camera after they finish a line.

Jack:	*(To Scott and Lily)* Tell us how you two have grown at home.
Scott:	Nothing can replace the wonderful church we go to. But Lily and I longed to have a closer fellowship with others in the church and wanted to grow stronger in our walk with God.
Lily:	We joined a Bible study group that meets once a week. I cannot tell you what a difference it has made in our lives. We have grown "at home" in ways that I cannot describe.
Scott:	We come together to study God's Word, share our burdens, share our joys, pray together, and enjoy close fellowship.
Lily:	This whole experience has given us a sense of belonging, caring, and even spiritual and emotional healing.
Bridget:	*(Thinks she has figured part of the conversation out)* Healing . . . like an aloe vera plant . . . but I thought you were a lily?
Brandon:	I must say we are a little surprised . . . but this venture seems like it has reaped a bountiful result. What do you contribute this harvest from?
Scott:	I contribute it to the miracle that God can do when we truly want to grow in all areas of our life.
Bridget:	Miracle Gro! Now I recognize that.
Jack:	A Christian who is deeply rooted in the Word of God, cultivated by a special group of caring people, and living in the *(pointing to sky)* "Son light" of Christ's love can blossom into a living witness, possessing the beauty of a rose, yet having the strength of the awesome redwood.
SOUND:	*HOME GROWN* THEME SONG (VERY LOW TO BEGIN)
Brandon:	Looks like our time is up. Jack, Scott, Lily, thank you for being here today and sharing your homegrown story with us. *(To audience)* Thank you for being with us here today and we hope you have enjoyed this program.
Bridget:	I still don't know how they got Lily in the ground!
Brandon:	Say good-bye, Bridget.
Bridget:	Good-bye, Bridget.
Brandon:	Good-bye. See you tomorrow on another edition of *The Home Grown Show.*
	(MUSIC SWELLS . . . GROUP BEGINS TO MINGLE)
LIGHTS:	**FADE TO BLACK**
	END

▸ *Caution: Gender-Specific Sketches*

When you have an all-male or all-female cast, be sure to steer clear of gender-specific generalizations. All women are not gossips, and all men are not insensitive. Allow your script to create the characterizations. Don't offend your audience's sensibilities by overgeneralizing.

▸ *Characterization: Bridget & Brandon Moment*

Bridget and Brandon are always "on"; we never see them when they are not performing. So whether it is to each other, their guests, or the camera, it's razzle-dazzle time!

HOME GROWN, TOO!

with Bridget & Brandon

TOPIC
Parents' responsibility in raising their children.

SYNOPSIS
The Home Grown Show with Bridget and Brandon is a morning talk show that features home improvement segments, gardening tips, and cooking demonstrations. *Home Grown* co-hosts Bridget and Brandon are never completely prepared for their guests, and today is no exception. Bridget and Brandon are under the impression that today's show is about gardening and caring for plants. They are surprised to find out that the show is actually about raising children.

SET/PROPS
Sketch takes place on a typical *Home Grown* set, decorated with flowers, books, plants, etc. A table or counter should be set up with gardening materials on it. Sketch can begin with a thirty- to sixty-second video/slide roll-in of Bridget and Brandon "show open" introduction set to a lively saxophone soundtrack. Applause track should be available.

CHARACTERS

Bridget – *Home Grown* co-host: exaggerated,
dramatic, airheaded and clueless

Brandon – *Home Grown* co-host: smooth,
charming, witty and conceited

Announcer – Introduces *The Home Grown Show* off-stage with microphone

Flora Graham – Child expert and author of
the book *Seedlings in the Storm*

Daisy Fields – Mother

Rocky Fields – Father

LIGHTS:	**BLACKOUT** *(Actors move into place)*
GRAPHIC:	**OPENING MUSIC/VIDEO SEGMENT FOR** *The Home Grown Show*

(If you have access to a video production crew, create a high-energy talk show opening sequence. The soundtrack should reflect a "talk show" feel. Show various poses of Bridget and Brandon around the set. Without video, create a slideshow of photos to develop the same effect.)

Announcer: *(Over trail of video . . . prerecorded or offstage microphone)* It's *Home Grown with Bridget and Brandon.* **(More music and video)** And here are our hosts, Bridget and Brandon!

LIGHTS: **LIGHTS UP – HOME GROWN SET**

(BRIDGET and BRANDON enter the overly decorated Home Grown set. They are dramatic, pretentious, and sparkling with enthusiasm.)

(NOTE: IF video camera is available, hosts should direct their first lines into the camera.)

Brandon: Welcome to another edition of *The Home Grown Show,* the daily home information talk show. Hi, I'm Brandon . . .

Bridget: . . . and I'm Bridget, and we have a wonderful show planned for you.

(BRIDGET and BRANDON turn to face audience)

Brandon: We're back in the garden today, and with some help from our very special guest, we'll learn what we can do to keep our plants from looking like this. **(Pulls a pathetically wilted plant out from behind the counter)**

Bridget: Did you grow that?

Brandon: *(Witty)* Yeah . . . all by myself. You should see the rest of my greenhouse!

Bridget: *(Giggling)* Brandon, now stop . . . I'm trying to do a show here.

Brandon: I can't help it . . . I'm the witty one.

Bridget: *(Picking up a beautiful silk flower)* We'll look at my prize (name of whatever flower is used).

Brandon: You grew this?

Bridget: I tell you, Brandon . . . I have the most miraculous green thumb. No matter what I do, it looks this good. If I overwater, if I underwater . . . it doesn't matter. Too much sun . . . not enough . . . no harm done. It's never had bugs and never has a leaf fallen off. Amazing, huh?

Brandon: *(Takes the plant and looks at it)* Bridget, this is a silk plant. It is artificial.

▶ *Drama Cue: Mix Types*

When a cast is made up of similar characters from a particular group of people (men or women, old or young, coworkers, Christians, etc.), mix types by combining physical statures, voice pitch, hair and eye color, speech patterns, and other distinguishing factors. Variety is the spice of life, especially onstage.

Bridget:	Oh, no wonder it never smelled very pretty.
Brandon:	We have a very special guest with us today. She is author of the new book *Seedlings in the Storm,* and we have invited her here to help us learn how we can grow *real* prize-winning plants. Help me welcome . . . Flora Graham!
MUSIC:	*HOME GROWN* THEME—MUSIC AND APPLAUSE
	(FLORA enters, is greeted by her hosts, and takes a stool.)
Brandon:	Flora, welcome to the show. First, I must apologize for Bridget and myself. We haven't had time to look at your book; we just returned from hosting the Vidal Sassoon Healthy Hair Days Telethon.
Bridget:	Oops! Sorry, Flora.
Brandon:	But we're guessing that *Seedlings in the Storm* is about . . . ?
Flora:	. . . the care and growth of little ones.
Bridget:	Those are the seedlings, I assume. So what are the storms?
Flora:	The storms are all the influences of this world that would squelch the growth and development of those seedlings.
Bridget:	Oh, that would be terrible. I love the taste of pumpkin seeds . . . sunflower seeds . . .
Flora:	Oh, I think you two are a little confused about the kind of seedlings I'm talking about. I'm not talking about seeds for flowers and plants, I'm talking about little ones . . . children.
Brandon & Bridget:	*(Dazed and confused)* Oh.
Flora:	Raising children today is a lot like planting and caring for flowers. They need proper care and attention or they will wilt.
Bridget:	Unless you get silk ones.
Brandon:	*(Ignoring her)* Go on, Flora.
	(DAISY and ROCKY FIELDS enter . . .)
Flora:	I have invited Daisy and Rocky Fields to join us today. Before the show, they told me they were having problems with their children.
Daisy:	That's right. Our seedlings have turned into stumps, I'm afraid.
Rocky:	Our manicured family has now turned into mulch.
Flora:	Do you spend time together as a family?
Daisy:	Sometimes. Every once in a while.
Flora:	Do you talk to your kids?

▶ *Caution:*
Prop-erty Created

A drama like this one asks for some pretty distinguishable props. Get creative. Take the time to create memorable props by using vivid colors, adding crafty designs, and paying attention to detail. The more interesting the prop, the better it will support the context of the drama.

Rocky:	Yeah. I'm usually telling them to leave me alone.
Flora:	Do you ever just sit down and talk with them?
Daisy:	Yeah, usually their teacher or principal is with us, but we are sitting down.
Bridget:	Well, at least your family can say it has "principals."
	(Everyone gives BRIDGET a puzzled stare)
Flora:	I would be interested to know what your dinner hour is like.
Daisy:	What's a dinner hour? Oh, you mean when we eat our evening meal. Well how should I describe it? Did you ever see *Raiders of the Lost Ark*?
Rocky:	Our house is like *Raiders of the Last PopTart!*
Flora:	Are there outside influences that you've noticed affecting your children?
Rocky:	Lots of them . . .
Daisy:	That's why we keep them inside the house where they can watch HBO, MTV, or listen to the radio.
Brandon:	So how are your children behaving? How are they doing?
Daisy:	Our five-year-old cries a lot and exclusively uses a black crayon when she colors. Our eight-year-old stares a lot and is making funny noises.
Rocky:	And our twelve-year-old says he hates his family and wishes he lived on the *Starship Enterprise*.
Bridget:	*(Trying to be chirpily positive)* Sounds like you have a wonderful family.
Brandon:	Flora, what is happening to the Fieldses' children?
Flora:	The storms of life are too great for your children. If they are going to blossom into strong healthy adults, you two need to take a little more time to care for and nurture them.
Daisy:	*(Perplexed)* I don't understand . . .
Flora:	*(Picking up a plant)* A seed is planted. It grows. With the right amount of water, sunlight, and oxygen, it can withstand the gusty gales of the wind and rain.
Rocky:	And what you're saying is that we need to give the right amount of love, discipline, understanding, and values to our children so they can withstand all the storms of life that will come their way.
Flora:	That's right.
Bridget:	*(Crying)* That is so touching!

▸ *Characterization: Bridget & Brandon Moment*

Bridget and Brandon are always in agreement. Have the co-hosts continue to add verbal agreements like "uh-huh," "oh yes," "gotcha," or "amazing" throughout the drama. These will be improvisational lines; place them strategically so they don't upstage another character's written dialogue.

MUSIC:	*HOME GROWN* THEME SONG BEGINS
Brandon:	Looks like our time is up. Flora, Rocky, Daisy, we thank you for being with us here today and sharing your homegrown stories with us.
	(To audience) Thank you for being with us, and we hope that you have enjoyed our program.
Bridget:	Are you sure this plant is silk? I am positive this plant has been growing.
Brandon:	Say good-bye, Bridget.
Bridget:	Good-bye, Bridget.
Brandon:	Good-bye, and we'll see you on the next edition of *The Home Grown Show.*
	(Music swells ... group begins to mingle ...)
LIGHTS:	**FADE TO BLACK**
	END

▶ *Characterization: Bridget & Brandon Moment*

Bridget and Brandon will sensationalize the most insignificant matter. So whether they are talking about something profound or transitioning to a commercial, have them deliver their lines with the utmost passion and panache.

© 2006 Paul Joiner - Please see page iv for more information.

HOME GROWN III
"Keep the Bible In"

TOPIC
Relevancy of the Bible in today's world

SYNOPSIS
The Home Grown Show with Bridget and Brandon is a morning talk show. Bridget and Brandon are larger-than-life celebrities who interview experts in a variety of interests. On today's show, our hosts have invited a team of experts from a mega-trend monitoring organization to present the New Year's list of what is in and what is out! Their list is entertaining—until we find that they have placed the Bible on the OUT list and put psychics, peer counseling, and talk shows on the IN list!

SETTING
Sketch takes place on the set of a home show. Sketch can begin with a pre-recorded video roll-in opening of *The Home Grown Show* with montage of video footage from previous shows.

CHARACTERS

Bridget – *Home Grown* co-host exaggerated, dramatic, pretentious, clueless but sincere

Brandon – *Home Grown* co-host: charming, very "Hollywood," pretentious but sincere

Announcer – Introduces *The Home Grown Show* off-stage with microphone

Yolanda – Guest on *Home Grown*: mega-trend expert

Kasha – Guest on *Home Grown*: mega-trend expert

LIGHTS:	**BLACKOUT** *(Actors move into place)*
GRAPHIC:	**OPENING MUSIC/VIDEO SEGMENT FOR** *The Home Grown Show*

(If you have access to a video production crew, create a high-energy talk show opening sequence. The soundtrack should reflect a "talk show" feel. Show various poses of Bridget and Brandon around the set. Without video, create a slideshow of photos to develop the same effect.)

Announcer: It's *Home Grown . . . with Bridget and Brandon . . .*

(MUSIC/VIDEO/OR SLIDES CONTINUE UNTIL . . .)

And here are your hosts . . . Bridget and Brandon!

LIGHTS:	**UP ON SET**
FOLLOW SPOTS:	**FOLLOW BRIDGET AND BRANDON IN**

(BRIDGET and BRANDON enter. Our co-hosts make a dramatic entrance, pausing to enjoy the applause)

Brandon: Welcome to another edition of *The Home Grown Show . . .* your daily home information talk show. I'm Brandon . . .

Bridget: And I'm Bridget, and we have a wonderful show planned for you today!

Don't we, Brandon?

Brandon: We sure do. Bridget, do you consider yourself "in"?

Bridget: In what? In a pickle? In a fix? In a bind? In-tertaining?

Brandon: No. Do you think you're . . . "with it"?

Bridget: I hope so. I'd rather be with it than without it. *(Pushing for a laugh)* Unless you're talking about a cold!

Brandon: Well, today we are going to find out if we are "with it" kind of people. Hey, you and I have always been in the "IN crowd," but I've invited some very special guests who will tell us what is IN and what is OUT in _____ *(insert current year.)*

Bridget: I know _____ is out! *(insert last year)*

Brandon: Well, let's find out if you're right. *(To audience)* Please help me welcome

Yolanda Speers and Kasha Green from Mega-Trends International!

SOUND:	*HOME GROWN THEME SONG*

(KASHA and YOLANDA enter. They are dressed very sharply and carry their IN and OUT lists in their hands. BRIDGET and BRANDON greet them and all four sit.)

▸ *Drama Cue:*
Physical Training

When your script calls for physical action to support dialogue, rehearse both—together! Your actors will actually recall their lines more easily when those lines are attached to specific actions.

Brandon:	Welcome to the show, Yolanda . . . Kasha! We're glad you could be here.
	So . . . we're dying to know, what's in and what's out?
Yolanda:	Well, before we get started, you'll be glad to know that home talk shows are IN right now!
Bridget:	That's a relief! *(Pushing for the laugh)* Job security!
Kasha:	Yolanda and I have been watching your show lately and agree that you two are very "in"!
Brandon:	*(Winking)* Man, I've been worried about that! So, we want to hear the list . . . what's in and what's out in (year)!
Yolanda:	We'll start with fashion. Black is out!
Kasha:	Bright colors are in . . . .orange, green, and lavender!
Bridget:	Yellow?
Kasha:	Very in!
Bridget:	Whew!
Yolanda:	Sixties' nostalgia is out!
Kasha:	But the seventies are in!
Brandon:	Good, I can keep wearing my mood ring!
Yolanda:	Our list includes business trends too. For instance, working at the office is out!
Kasha:	Telecommuting from home is in!
Yolanda:	And while we're at home, you'll want to know that video games are out!
Kasha:	Multimedia centers are in!
Bridget:	Shame on me. I still have an eight-track, can you believe it?
Brandon:	Where is everyone traveling to nowadays?
Yolanda:	Trips to Europe are out!
Kasha:	Trips to Amazon rain forests are in.
Yolanda:	Society is changing and evolving so quickly now. People tend to be more self-confident, more in touch with their feelings . . . .
Bridget:	For example . . .
Yolanda:	Values are out!
Kasha:	Television and radio tabloid shows are in!
Yolanda:	Guilt is out!

▸ *Characterization: Bridget & Brandon Moment*

Bridget and Brandon are always playing to the camera. Their big smiles, tilting of their heads, pointing, winking, and other physical quirks will help you create truly cheesy television talk-show hosts.

Kasha:	Trusting in your decisions is in!
Yolanda:	Church is out!
Bridget:	Even on Sunday?
Kasha:	Yes. Peer support is in!
Yolanda:	Pastoral counseling is out!
Kasha:	Psychic hotlines are in.
Yolanda:	The Bible is out!
Kasha:	Self-improvement books are in!
Brandon:	Wait! Did you say that the Bible is out? *The Bible?* The number one bestselling book of all time, the book that still remains on the top ten list is out?
Yolanda:	That's what they say.
Brandon:	Who's they?
Yolanda:	You know . . . "them"!
Brandon:	I'd love to know who they are, because they are really out of line on this one.
Kasha:	The Bible isn't really relevant in the twenty-first century.
Bridget:	*(Confused)* Wait, but I thought the seventies were in.
Kasha:	The archaic teachings of the Bible aren't practical anymore.
Yolanda:	That's why the Bible is on its way out.
Brandon:	Your list was pretty accurate until you put the Bible on the Out list. You better go back and do your homework.
Yolanda:	Sorry, we have, and the Bible is OUT!
Bridget:	*(Pretentious)* No . . . you two are out! We've run out of time! And you're out of here!
	(BRIDGET and BRANDON walk to center stage and address audience)
MUSIC:	*HOME GROWN* THEME
Brandon:	Thank you for joining us today. We hope you're in style, in touch, in the groove, and in the swing of things after seeing today's show. But please don't make the mistake of . . .
Bridget:	. . . taking the Bible out of your life!
Brandon:	Join us again tomorrow for the *The Home Grown Show.* Say good-bye, Bridget.
Bridget:	Good-bye, Bridget.

▸ *Caution: Fashion Alert*

When a drama has a setting that calls for a type of clothing you wouldn't normally see in a church service (i.e., gym clothes, pajamas, beachwear, etc.), make sure that final costumes are preapproved before actors take the stage. Pay heed to modesty and appropriateness. Also, be sure to eliminate costume choices that have inappropriate words or logos printed on garments.

Brandon: And I'm Brandon, good-bye!

(BRIDGET and BRANDON smile at the audience and wave. KASHA and YOLANDA seem to be very uncomfortable . . . begin picking up their things and leave . . .)

LIGHTS: **FADE TO BLACK**

END

▸ *Characterization: Bridget & Brandon Moment*

Bridget and Brandon live in color—don't forget to add color to everything they do. Their clothes, coffee cups, props, and other accessories should scream for attention.

Home Grown

THIS IS YOUR TITHE

with Bridget and Brandon

TOPIC
Tithing/investing in the lives of others

SYNOPSIS
Bridget and Brandon are hosts of the talk show *The Home Grown Show with Bridget and Brandon,* which focuses on the "family of God" and the "home" we call church. On today's program, they are honoring a man for his faithfulness in tithing in the style of the old television program *This Is Your Life.* We'll see how many lives have been affected by his commitment to tithing over the years.

SETTING
Stage should look like that of a talk show. A chair sits center stage, and a platform should be placed a few feet behind the chair.

CHARACTERS

Bridget – *Home Grown* co-host; exaggerated and dramatic; clueless

Brandon – *Home Grown* co-host; handsome; obnoxiously charming; likes himself

Announcer – Introduces *The Home Grown Show* off-stage with microphone

David Lynn – Tither

Pastor Howard – David's pastor

Jimmy Kelt – David's former Sunday school student

Flora Johnson – Missionary supported by David's tithe

Barbara Lynn – David's wife

Organist – For dramatic effect (if no organist or keyboardest is available, have your sound technician create the cues.)

LIGHTS:	**BLACKOUT** *(Actors move into place)*
GRAPHIC:	**OPENING MUSIC/VIDEO SEGMENT FOR** *The Home Grown Show*
	(If you have access to a video production crew, create a high-energy talk show opening sequence. The soundtrack should reflect a "talk show" feel. Show various poses of Bridget and Brandon around the set. Without video, create a slideshow of photos to develop the same effect.)
Announcer:	***(When name of program is on screen)*** It's *The Home Grown Show with Bridget and Brandon.*
	And now, your hosts—Bridget and Brandon!
SOUND:	**APPLAUSE**
	(BRIDGET and BRANDON enter, charismatically waving and greeting the audience.)
Brandon:	Welcome to another edition of *The Home Grown Show.* I'm Brandon . . .
Bridget:	. . . and I'm Bridget, and we have a wonderful show planned for you today. ***(Realizing that she has forgotten what the show is about)*** Wait, what is today's show about?
Brandon:	We have a very special show today, because we are honoring a man who has for years been faithfully investing his life in the lives of others.
Bridget:	He must be a banker?
Brandon:	No.
Bridget:	A teacher?
Brandon:	No . . . a tither.
Bridget:	That's right.
Brandon:	His name is David Lynn. ***(To the audience)*** Won't you help me welcome him to the show?
SOUND:	*HOME SHOW* **THEME SONG WITH APPLAUSE**
	(DAVID enters stage. Looks a little uneasy)
Brandon:	David welcome to *The Home Grown Show.* You're probably wondering why you are here today.
David:	Yes, I am.
Brandon:	David, you have been faithful tithing in your local church for years, and we want to honor you today with a special edition of our show called "This Is Your Tithe."
SOUND:	**THEME SONG SHOULD BE PLAYED WHEN BRANDON MENTIONS "THIS IS YOUR TITHE."**

▸ *Drama Cue:*
The Word for Today

The slang of today should not be used in the dialogue of yesteryear. Actors' reactions and improvisational responses to dialogue should be well thought-out and appropriate for the time and place in which the drama occurs.

GRAPHIC:	SLIDE— *This Is Your Tithe*
Bridget:	Now David, if you will just sit right here. We have assembled a few people who have been directly touched by your tithes and offerings. And they are here to tell you what your faithfulness has meant to them.
	(As BRIDGET speaks the previous line, PASTOR HOWARD, JIMMY, FLORA, and BARBARA enter and stand on the platform with their backs to the audience.)
ORGAN:	**BACKGROUND TO PASTOR's TALK ...** **CONTINUES THROUGHOUT ALL THE TRIBUTES)**
Pastor:	*(Turns around)* David, you are every pastor's dream and every church's security. Your faithfulness in giving has been an example to all of us who have observed your life. Our church is strong because of men like you.
Brandon:	David, do you know who that is?
David:	I'd know that voice anywhere ... I hear it every Sunday. It's my pastor, Pastor Howard.
SOUND	*(ORGAN SWELLS)*
	(PASTOR comes down and is reunited with DAVID)
Pastor:	David, a big thank-you from all of us at First Community Church.
David:	Thank you.
	(DAVID sits back down ... PASTOR steps to the side)
Bridget:	And what about this voice from the past?
Jimmy:	*(Turns to audience)* Dear Brother Dave. It was because of your tithe and your commitment to the children's program at our church that I found the Lord. You picked me up every Sunday and took me to church with your family, and I was in your Sunday school class. No telling where I'd be today without your faithfulness.
Brandon:	David?
David:	Could it be little Jimmy Kelt?
Brandon:	It's Jimmy, but he's not so little anymore. Jimmy, come on down.
David:	Jimmy? You're bigger than me.
Jimmy:	Bro. Dave. I want to thank you for investing your time and your money in my life.
	(DAVID and JIMMY hug. JIMMY stands to the side.)
Bridget:	We have some one else who wants to tell you about the investment you've made in her life.

▸ *Characterization:*
Bridget & Brandon
Moment

The co-hosts can be a little dense. Without cracking a smile, Bridget and Brandon are sometimes very confused and often don't "get it." Nevertheless, they're Bridget and Brandon! It's their show, so who cares?

▸ *Caution: Costume*
Adjustments

Allow plenty of time for your actors to adjust to their costumes before your performance. This will allow your actors to get comfortable with the way the costumes feel and look. Types of clothes not normally worn by your actors (especially period costumes) can distract them from concentrating on their lines.

Flora:	*(Turns to audience. She is carrying a photo album in her hand.)* David, we have never met, but we both agree on the importance of missions. You see, I live on the other side of the world and work as a missionary in India. It is because your faithful giving that I am able to remain on the field and reach the lost for Christ.
Bridget:	David, meet Miss Flora Johnson.
SOUND:	*ORGAN SWELLS*
	(DAVID and FLORA embrace. FLORA holds up the photo album)
Flora:	David, I want you to have this photo album full of pictures of the men and women who have come to know the Lord because of our mission. Thank you.
Brandon:	Now David, there is someone else in your life who has been touched by your tithe.
Barbara:	David, you have been a godly example to the children and me in the area of tithing. Your leadership and faith in God's promise to provide our every need is an inspiration to all of us. We love you.
ORGAN:	**ORGAN SWELLS**
	(BRIDGET motions for BARBARA to join her husband. They embrace.)
Brandon:	*(To DAVID)* David, did you realize how far-reaching your tithe really was?
	(All those who honored DAVID stand behind his chair)
David:	No. It's wonderful to see.
Bridget:	Anything you would like to say to someone who is thinking about tithing?
David:	The commitment is worth it. The investment, eternal!
SOUND:	*BRIDGET AND BRANDON THEME SONG*
Brandon:	Well that's all the time we have for today. Join us tomorrow when we talk about eternal investments.
Bridget:	External investments? You're talking about vitamin supplements and cosmetic surgery?
Brandon:	Not external . . . *eternal* investments! *(To audience)* See you then. Say good night, Bridget . . .
Bridget:	*(Clueless)* Good night, Bridget . . . .
Brandon:	Bye-bye!
	(Group gathers together and visits as . . .)
LIGHTS:	**FADE TO BLACK**
	END

▶ *Characterization: Bridget & Brandon Moment*

Talk about exaggerating! Rachel and Roger are the ultimate. If it is an inch, it is a mile! If it is good, it's the greatest! Identify the dialogue where Bridget and Brandon are concerned more about good ratings than they are the truth . . . and then milk it for all it's worth.

What Was That? Who's There?
IT'S CECIL & PENELOPE!

Cecil and Penelope have been capturing the hearts of audiences for years. They'll make you laugh and cry. You'll be amazed at their wisdom and humbled by their grateful hearts. They own nothing, yet have everything. They are homeless but looking forward to the day they move into their mansion.

Cecil and Penelope are part of the family at my church. In fact, a holiday without these two showing up is not a holiday at all. They receive cheers from our congregation before they even say a word. Why? Because our congregation knows that when Cecil and Penelope walk onstage, they are going to be profoundly moved by the couple's simple and childlike message.

You'll find three Cecil and Penelope sketches in this volume of *Life Scripts* and a few more in the other *Life Scripts for the Church* volumes. Here is a little more about Cecil and Penelope to help you re-create the same endearing characters in your church.

Wardrobe

Cecil and Penelope are homeless, so their costumes should look like clothing the two have either been given or found. Smudges of dirt may be seen on their faces as well as their clothes, which are ragged, torn, and somewhat dirty. However, don't make them look unkempt . . . just a little messy.

Demeanor

Cecil and Penelope's mental condition should not be overdone to a degree that it distracts from their dialogue, nor should their actions resemble anything like making fun of the mentally disabled. The couple's mental disability does not manifest itself in crazy behavior; it simply makes them charming, innocent, endearing, and comically childlike.

Set

Cecil and Penelope live in the city park. You can create their "home" with a few artificial trees, two park benches, and a trash can. We usually find Cecil and Penelope in the same place in every drama.

Paul's Favorites

Cecil and Penelope are definitely my favorite characters. They are so real, simple, vulnerable, and pure. I have learned a lot from this homeless couple, and your church will, too. The following are my three favorite Cecil & Penelope sketches:

Little Baby What's-His-Name / *Life Scripts: Holidays*
You've Got to Say It / *Life Scripts: Characters*
The Grand Opening: Easter / *Life Scripts: Holidays*

Cecile and Penelope would love to meet you. Check out the original Cecil and Penelope at www.pauljoiner.com and get some ideas for re-creating them in your own church.

And now . . . the queen and king of the city park, Cecil and Penelope!

THE COUNTING GAME

with Cecil and Penelope

TOPIC
God's goodness/counting our blessings in times of trouble

SYNOPSIS
Cecil and Penelope, a homeless street couple, bring spiritual enlightenment to people they encounter at the park where they live. A young couple laments the rough circumstances in their life. They have come to the point where they are even questioning if God really cares for them at all. After Cecil and Penelope arrive and find this troubled couple, they share with them a game they call the Counting Game. After a little instruction, they take the couple through the game of counting their blessings. The game changes the young couple's hearts and attitudes and replaces their bitterness with a sense of thankfulness.

SETS/PROPS
This sketch takes place in a park: trees, two park benches, and a trash can will set the scene of the park. Penelope and Cecil carry plastic pages filled with the "treasures" they have found. Penelope's bag of treasures should include an old tattered hymnal.

CHARACTERS

August – husband

Jacey – wife

Cecil – homeless, mentally disabled

Penelope – homeless, mentally disabled

NOTE: *Cecil and Penelope's mental condition should not be acted out to a degree that it distracts from their dialogue, nor should their actions be viewed as offensive. The couple's mental disability does not manifest itself in "crazy" behavior as much as it makes them charming, innocent, endearing, and comically childlike.*

LIGHTS:	BLACKOUT *(Actors move into place)*
SOUND:	MUSICAL TRANSITION INTO SKETCH
GRAPHIC:	TITLE SLIDE— *The Counting Game*
LIGHTS:	UP ON STAGE

(We see AUGUST and JACEY in the park. AUGUST sits on a park bench with his head in his hands. JACEY is standing SR looking off into the distance. Both appear very distraught.)

Jacey: So what are we going to do, August?

August: I told you. I don't *know* what we should do.

Jacey: It just seems that it's been one disaster after another.

August: It seems that way.

Jacey: So when is it all going to end? Haven't we had more than our share of trouble?

August: *(Standing)* Look, honey, we just have to hang in there.

Jacey: We've been hanging in there for a long, long time. *(Sitting)* And you know what I can't help but thinking?

August: *(Sitting down next to JACEY on the bench)* I know what you're going to say: "Where is God in all this?"

Jacey: I hate feeling this way, but I thought God was supposed to be good to His children.

August: It's like we've been abandoned.

Jacey: Can you think of a worse life than ours?

(CECIL and PENELOPE enter carrying their garbage bags. The two couples notice each other. JACEY and AUGUST grow a little uncomfortable at the sight of the street couple.)

Cecil: Look, Penelope—visitors!

Penelope: We love visitors!

Cecil: Hello, my name is Cecil and this is Penelope. And we live here in the park.

Penelope: In fact, you are sitting right smack-dab in the middle of our lovely living area.

August: Oh, I'm sorry. We'll leave.

Penelope: Don't leave.

▶ *Drama Cue:*
Creating a Scene

Coming up with a few well-placed set pieces is sometimes better than creating an entire detailed set. Is your drama in a park? Set it with an artificial potted tree and a bench. On a street corner? Use a trash can, bench, and a street sign.

Cecil:	What is your names?
August:	My name is August, and this is my wife . . .
Penelope:	Let me guess . . . September!
August:	No, this is Jacey.
Penelope:	Jacey. What a pretty name.
August:	You really live here in the park?
Cecil:	Sure do. Aren't we lucky to have such a beautiful home? Trees, birds, skunks, picnic tables, sprinkler systems that we can run through on a hot day, and fun people like you that we get to meet.
Penelope:	We have a great life, don't we? How about you? You must have a wonderful life, too!
Jacey:	Well, since you asked, our life stinks!
Cecil:	Our life stinks sometimes, too, that's why we have to run through the sprinklers as much as we can.
August:	What my wife means is that our life couldn't get any worse. I've been laid off from work . . .
Jacey:	My job situation isn't the best . . .
August:	We're trying to qualify to buy a home . . .
Jacey:	We're having trouble with my parents . . .
August:	I've been having some heath problems . . .
Jacey:	And we're a little mad at God!
Penelope:	Mad at God? What did He do?
Jacey:	It appears He isn't doing anything!
August:	I guess if anyone can understand what it is to have such a miserable existence, it would be you two!
	(A brief silence as CECIL and PENELOPE look at each other)
Cecil:	The Counting Game. Penelope, get the hymnikal!
	(PENELOPE begins to root through her bag to find the hymnal)
	Would you like to play a game? I think it would make you feel better.
Jacey:	A game?

▶ *Caution: Prop Prep*

When preparing for a prop-intensive drama, take time on the details. The props are the true stars of this kind of sketch, so be sure to find or design the right ones. Don't wait until the last minute to start looking for what you need.

Cecil:	It's called the Counting Game. Penelope and I made it up.
Penelope:	You see, Cecil and I found this old hymnal in the garbage one day. We don't know how the songs go, but the words sure are wonderful!
Cecil:	I can't read, so Penelope has to read the hymnikal to me and one day she read . . . Read it, Penelope . . .
Penelope:	It's called, "Count Your Many Blessings," and it goes like this:
	(She reads)
	Are you ever burdened with a load of care?
	Does the cross seem heavy you are called to bear?
	Count your many blessings every doubt will fly
	And you will be singing as the days go by.
Cecil:	*(Taking over saying the words by memory)*
	Count your blessings name them one by one.
	Count your blessings see what God has done.
Penelope:	So whenever we feel a little down, we play the Counting Game and see how many blessings we can count.
Cecil:	One time we counted sixty-four blessings we could be thankful for.
	Can you just believe it?
Jacey:	Sixty-four? We could never count sixty-four things to be thankful for.
Penelope:	I bet you could.
SOUND:	**MUSICAL BACKGROUND BEGINS**
	Number one is sitting right next to you.
	(JACEY and AUGUST look at one another)
	So you both go like this. *(PENELOPE holds up one finger . . . and JACEY and AUGUST follow her lead)*
Cecil:	And wait . . . listen . . . I hear number two? It's your hearts beating. You're alive. That's a blessing.
	(Everyone holds up two fingers . . . and continue this with every blessing counted.)
Penelope:	And look at your pretty, pretty clothes. Number three!

▸ *Characterization: Cecil & Penelope Moment*

Cecil and Penelope are people persons. They love guests and always want them to feel welcome in "their park." These two are shy at first, but their smiles never fade. It should be like a breath of fresh air whenever they appear.

Cecil:	And shoes!
	(Four fingers)
Penelope:	And pretty jewelry.
	(Five fingers)
Cecil:	Did you get to have breakfast?
	(A humbled JACEY and AUGUST both nod.)
	Wow, that's a blessing you had that we never get to have.
	(Six fingers)
Penelope:	You have a place to live . . .
Cecil:	With real showers . . .
	(Seven fingers)
Penelope:	And a real bed is softer than a picnic table.
	(Eight fingers)
Cecil:	And at least you have a family.
Penelope:	We don't.
	(Nine fingers. Grows silent)
Cecil:	And that's how you play the Counting Game.
SOUND:	**MUSIC BACKGROUND FADES OUT**
August:	Jacey, they are so right. We have been focusing on the bad and not seeing the good. We have a wonderful life in spite of our problems.
Jacey:	And we've been blaming everything on God.
Penelope:	Don't blame the bad things on God . . . just the good things.
Cecil:	If all I had in the whole wide world to count as a blessing was only Penelope, then God would be good.
August:	*(Standing)* Cecil, Penelope, thank you for teaching us to play the Counting Game when we are going through bad times. It is something that we will never forget.
Jacey:	I see things very differently now. I can be thankful for God's goodness in the midst of our troubles.
August:	Thank you.
SOUND:	**MUSICAL TRANSITION OUT OF SKETCH**
Cecil:	Oh, I just thought of another blessing for you to count. Be thankful you are not us.
	(A brief moment of sober silence)

Jacey: No, I can't count that blessing because in many ways I wish we were more like you.

(AUGUST and JACEY are visually moved by their encounter with CECIL and PENELOPE. They begin to exit, then stop, look at one another, and turn back to CECIL and PENELOPE. They slowly point to CECIL, then raise one finger ... and then to PENELOPE, and raise another finger ... then smile and leave. CECIL and PENELOPE watch them go, then turn to each other and nod their heads ... they are going to play the Counting Game. PENELOPE starts by looking upward to God ... they both nod in agreement and raise one finger. They both point to the park in which they live ... and raise a second finger. CECIL points to PENELOPE and raises a third finger ... and she does the same to him. PENELOPE motions to her clothes ... CECIL agrees ... and they hold up four fingers. CECIL then takes his finger and runs it across PENELOPE's big smile ... and holds up five fingers. PENELOPE blushes, then reaches up and kisses CECIL on the top of his head ... and holds up six fingers ... CECIL is delighted and reaches out his hand to PENELOPE ... and before they take hands and hug they both raise seven fingers. They embrace ...)

LIGHTS: FADE TO BLACK

   END

▸ *Characterization: Cecil & Penelope Moment*

There is a pattern to Cecil and Penelope: They greet; they listen; they share; and then they receive. Establish this pattern consistently in every Cecil & Penelope sketch.

FEED MY LAMBS
With Cecil and Penelope

TOPIC
Ministry: Simple people who do amazing things for God.

SYNOPSIS
Cecil and Penelope, a homeless street couple, stumble upon a young couple who are on their way to take the pastorate of a small church in a neighboring town. The young couple are feeling less than confident about becoming the leaders of this church. Cecil and Penelope remind them that God has called them to be shepherds and all they need to do is "feed His lambs." In spite of Cecil and Penelope telling them that God uses simple people to do amazing things, the couple still feels inadequate. Finally, in their own unique way, Cecil and Penelope show the couple how they should face the ministry before them.

CHARACTERS

Michael – young minister

Rachel – young minister's wife

Cecil – homeless man; mentally disabled; companion to Penelope

Penelope – homeless woman; mentally disabled; companion to Cecil

NOTE: *Cecil and Penelope's mental condition should not be acted out to a degree that it distracts from their dialogue, nor should their actions be viewed as offensive. The couple's mental disability does not manifest itself in "crazy" behavior as much as it makes them charming, innocent, endearing, and comically childlike.*

SETS/PROPS
Sketch takes place in the city park: two trees, two park benches, and a trash can will help replicate the park feel. Cecil and Penelope should carry a few bags with their belongings in them. Michael and Rachel should have a Bible and a briefcase with them.

LIGHTS:	BLACKOUT *(Actors move into places)*
SOUND:	MUSICAL TRANSITION INTO SKETCH
GRAPHIC:	TITLE SLIDE— *Feed My Lambs*
LIGHTS:	LIGHTS UP ON STAGE

► *Drama Cue:*
Serious Fun

Lighthearted dramas require the actors to have FUN while performing. Train your actors to embrace comedy. As you rehearse, remind your cast that their objective is to stimulate laughter and goodwill.

(MICHAEL and RACHEL are in the city park. RACHEL sits on the park bench and MICHAEL is pacing. On the bench next to RACHEL is a Bible. A briefcase is beside the bench.)

Rachel: Michael, we can't stay here forever.

Michael: I know.

Rachel: Look, honey, I'm scared too, but we've already made a commitment to those people. *(She realizes MICHAEL's state of mind)* You're not thinking about . . .

Michael: *(Crossing to RACHEL and sitting down)* Rachel, we could call them. Tell them that we were on our way and we changed our mind.

(RACHEL looks at the ground . . .)

I just don't think I'm ready.

Rachel: I don't think I'm ready, either. But will we ever be?

Michael: What if I can't do it? I mean, who am I to pastor a church?

Rachel: We've been called to the ministry, Mike. And we've been to Bible school.

Michael: Maybe that's not enough.

Rachel: But is there anything else you'd rather do than preach?

Michael: No. Still, I think maybe we're way over our head with this one. *(Takes RACHEL's hand)* Just give me a minute to think.

Rachel: Maybe we shouldn't be sitting here. This park doesn't look very safe.

(CECIL and PENELOPE, a homeless couple that live in the park, enter carrying the few possessions they have in plastic trash bags)

Cecil: Look Penelope, we have visitors!

Penelope: What a lovely, lovely couple!

(RACHEL and MICHAEL don't know what to make of these odd characters)

Cecil: Hello, my name is Cecil and this is Penelope. And we live here in the park.

© 2006 Paul Joiner - Please see page iv for more information.

Rachel:	Oh, we're sorry. Is this your bench?
Penelope:	No. Today it's your bench!
Cecil:	I don't know who, but someone has a very, very pretty Bible.
Michael:	Oh, this is our Bible.
Penelope:	Wow, you're so lucky to have a Bible.
Michael:	We have lots of Bibles. Uh, my name is Michael and this is my wife, Rachel.
Cecil:	Hello. We used to have a kiddie Bible, but then one day someone stole it.
Penelope:	You have a beautiful Bible, so why are you so sad?
Rachel:	We're not sad. We're just worried.
Penelope:	About what?
Michael:	My wife and I are traveling across the state to become the new pastors of a small country church in a town not too far from here.
Rachel:	But we stopped here at the park because we're having second thoughts.
Michael:	I don't think I have what it takes to be a good pastor.
Rachel:	And I worry that I don't have what it takes to be a good pastor's wife.
Cecil:	Oh no, look at you. You're perfect. God uses simple people to do big, amazing things for Him!
Penelope:	We see that happen every day!
Michael:	*(Motioning to his briefcase)* I've just finished seminary; I have all the right books. But I just don't know how to be a pastor.
SOUND:	**MUSICAL BACKGROUND**
Penelope:	Do you know what a pastor really is?
Michael:	No. What?
Penelope:	A shepherd. You and you are going to be shepherds.
Cecil:	And you do you know what shepherds are supposed to do?
Rachel:	What?
Cecil:	Feed the lambs.
Michael:	That's right. Christ said, "Feed my sheep."
Penelope:	It's easy, 'cause lambs only eat a little bit at a time. A nibble here, a nibble there.

▸ *Characterization:*
Cecil & Penelope
Moment

Cecil and Penelope
know that they are not
"all there," but they also
know that they are
complete in Christ.
In other words, their
childlike behavior
always turns into
heavenly wisdom.
Allow the transitions
from their innocence
to their knowledge
to be subtle but
distinctive. Do this
with body language,
vocal expressions,
and gestures.

Cecil:	And do you know what lambs eat?
Rachel:	No, what do they eat?
Cecil:	Hey.
Rachel:	Hay?
Penelope:	So when you become shepherds, just feed your lambs hey.
Michael:	I don't get it. How do I feed my sheep hay?
Cecil:	It's simple. You just say, "Hey, Jesus loves you."
Penelope:	"Hey, everything will be okay. Jesus is here."
Cecil:	"Hey, don't cry. One day you'll see your mother in heaven."
Penelope:	"Hey, can I pray with you?"
Cecil:	And that's how you feed your lambs hey.
	(MICHAEL and RACHEL are hit hard by the simple message. They look at one another . . .)
Michael:	*(Emotional)* I think we could do that.
	(RACHEL can't speak but nods her head "yes")
	MUSIC FADES
Cecil:	Some people say hey is for horses, but it's not.
Penelope:	Hey is for lambs and sheep.
Cecil:	A shepherd just picks hey each Sunday. That's all.
Michael:	Wow, all of a sudden I think I can be a pastor. *(Stands, picks up his briefcase, and walks CS)* Start out small, one "hey" at a time. Who knows, maybe one day I'll preach in a big church, or on the radio, or on television.
Rachel:	*(Stand next to him)* Just one hey at a time, there, Michael.
Michael:	So do you think we're ready to do this, Rachel?
Rachel:	Yes.
	(CECIL and PENELOPE stand on either side of them . . .)
Cecil:	Oh no, you're not ready yet.
Penelope:	You've got too much baggage.
Cecil:	*(Bleating like a sheep)* Baaaa-gage.
Penelope:	We'll help you get ready.

SOUND:	MUSICAL TRANSITION OUT OF SKETCH

(Gently, PENELOPE takes MICHAEL's briefcase out of his hand and sets it to the side. CECIL then takes MICHAEL's coat off and lays it on the bench. PENELOPE has taken the Bible from the bench and put it in MICHAEL's hand. CECIL and PENELOPE take the couple's hands and join them together. MICHAEL and RACHEL are looking straight ahead. CECIL and PENELOPE smile at each other, then gently they raise the couple's heads until they are looking to the heavens. CECIL and PENELOPE remove their hands and the couple stands hand in hand with their heads lifted to heaven.)

Cecil: Now you're ready.

(RACHEL and MICHAEL remain there for a moment, then look at each other and smile.)

Michael: We'd better go. We have some lambs waiting for us.

(RACHEL and MICHAEL collect their things, hug CECIL and PENELOPE, and whisper their good-byes. MICHAEL and RACHEL begin to exit the stage and then turn to CECIL and PENELOPE.

Michael: Hey . . .

(CECIL and PENELOPE turn to the couple . . .)

You know when you said that God uses simple people to do amazing things? You were right. Thank you.

(MICHAEL hands CECIL and PENELOPE the Bible, then he and RACHEL exit. CECIL and PENELOPE walk to CS, hold the Bible, hold hands, and then in the same manner as they showed RACHEL and MICHAEL turn their heads up to the heavens . . .)

LIGHTS: FADE TO BLACK

END

▸ *Characterization: Cecil & Penelope Moment*

Background music plays a big role in Cecil & Penelope dramas. Find sensitive and emotional instrumental selections to underscore their "wisdom" dialogue in the script.

"You Gotta Say It!"

with Cecil and Penelope

TOPIC

Thanksgiving: Telling special people in our lives that we're thankful for them.

SYNOPSIS

An adult brother and sister are escaping the "madness" of a Thanksgiving celebration where family is in abundant supply. Upon stopping at the city park, their paths cross with Cecil and Penelope, a homeless and somewhat mentally disabled couple. As usual, these lowly street people bring a little laughter to the brother and sister, and in the process humbly teach them the importance of telling those you are thankful for how much you appreciate them . . . before the chance is gone.

SET/PROPS

Sketch takes place in a public park. Trees, two benches, and a trash can could be used to set the stage. The brother and sister need to have grocery bags . . . canned goods, milk, pies, etc. Cecil and Penelope carry belongings with them, and in Penelope's bag is a special "Thanksgiving box" with scraps of paper. Two Styrofoam "to-go" food containers are needed.

CHARACTERS

Rob – adult brother to Dorine

Dorine – adult sister to Rob

Cecil – homeless, mentally disabled man

Penelope – homeless, mentally disabled woman

NOTE: *Cecil and Penelope's mental condition should not be acted out to a degree that it distracts from their dialogue, nor should their actions be viewed as offensive. The couple's mental disability does not manifest itself in "crazy" behavior as much as it makes them charming, innocent, endearing, and comically childlike.*

LIGHTS:	**BLACKOUT** (*Actors move into place*)
SOUND:	**MUSIC TRANSITION INTO SKETCH**
GRAPHIC:	**TITLE SLIDE—** *"You Gotta Say It!"*
LIGHTS:	**UP ON STAGE**

(ROB and DORINE enter the park next to the park benches . . .)

Rob: Are you ready to go back?

Dorine: Honestly? No.

Rob: I say we hang out here for a few more minutes . . . they won't be missing us yet.

(Sit together on the bench)

Dorine: Hmm . . . just listen.

Rob: What do you hear?

Dorine: Nothing. No children. No one barking orders about how the turkey should be carved. No everyone talking at once.

Rob: Aha . . . that's why you were so quick to volunteer to walk to the store with me.

Dorine: You got it . . . I had to get out of there. I love our family, Rob . . . and Mom outdid herself with the Thanksgiving dinner, but . . .

Rob: I know, sis. Sometimes family can really get on your nerves . . . especially on the holidays!

Dorine: That's what I didn't want to say . . . but you're right.

Rob: *(Thinking)* You know, it would be nice to spend a peaceful Thanksgiving somewhere off by yourself . . . a place where you could have all the white meat you wanted.

Dorine: Yeah . . . a place where you wouldn't have to fix the children's plates first. A place where no one would bother you . . .

(CECIL and PENELOPE enter carrying Styrofoam to-go food containers)

Cecil: *(Seeing DORINE and ROB)* Oh . . . Happy Thanksgiving,

Penelope: Happy Thanksgiving!

Cecil: *(Pointing to the grocery bags)* Oh look, Penelope, they're bag people just like us!

Penelope: *(Referring to their own Styrofoam containers)* Hey, they're giving out Thanksgiving dinners at the mission! You should go get some!

Cecil: Yeah! It's free. There's turkey, and dressing . . . and the red stuff . . . and smashed potatoes—but they ran out of pumpkin pie . . . can you believe it . . . no pumpkin pie left!

▸ *Drama Cue:*
One with the Audience

Characters in a script often represent the different ways in which people view and act on a certain subject. Help your actors understand that the audience will be able to identify with their character if they express authenticity and vulnerability.

Penelope:	But we're thankful anyway, right, Cecil?
Cecil:	Yes . . . pumpkin pie is not that big of deal.
Penelope:	You better hurry and get to the mission before they run out!
Rob:	Thank you, but my sister and I have already had our Thanksgiving dinner.
Dorine:	We ran out of a few things and were sent to the store.
Penelope:	*(Sitting)* Oh . . . so you had a real live Thanksgiving dinner?
Dorine:	Yes, we did.
Penelope:	You're so lucky.
Cecil:	Very lucky.
Rob:	Listen, why don't we leave you two alone so you can eat.
Cecil:	Oh that's all right. You can stay. We never eat Thanksgiving dinner until we do our Thanksgiving transition.
Penelope:	Tradition . . .
Cecil:	Right . . . tradition . . . tradition . . . Thanksgiving tradition!
Dorine:	And what is that?
Penelope:	I'll show you.

(PENELOPE reaches into her bag and pulls out an old battered box)

It's our Thanksgiving box.

Cecil:	It's full of stuff that Penelope and I are thankful for. We write 'em down on paper.
Penelope:	*(Aside to DORINE)* I write them down . . . Cecil can't write . . .
Rob:	So, show us how your Thanksgiving box works.
Cecil:	Okay . . . I'll go first . . .

(CECIL reaches into the box and pulls out a tattered piece of paper. He looks at it as if he reads it . . . then nonchalantly shows it to PENELOPE.)

Penelope:	*(Looks at the others)* Cecil can't read, either. *(Reading to CECIL)* Our home.
Cecil:	I am thankful for this park where we live. I thank God for giving us such a beautiful place to live. And today I will thank the man who takes care of this park.
Penelope:	I'll go next. *(She draws a paper)* Clothes. I am thankful for the clothes we get at the mission. I will find old Charlotte and thank her for always giving us our clothes.

▸ *Caution: Eye Level*

Sometimes a drama has lines calling for an actor to speak outward and upward to God. The best way to do this is to choose a spot above the audience that conveys the idea of looking heavenward. Just don't position your head too far upward, or all the audience will see is your neck and nostrils. Let them see your eyes!

Cecil:	C'mon, you try it.
Rob:	Dorine, pick one for both of us.
Dorine:	Okay . . .
	(She pulls out a tattered piece of paper . . . has a hard time reading it, then figures the writing out . . .)
	Family. *(She looks at ROB)*
Rob:	You're kidding . . .
Penelope:	You do have families?
Dorine:	Yes . . . we do.
Cecil:	With kids, and grandpas and moms and dads?
Rob:	Yes . . .
Cecil:	You're so lucky.
Penelope:	You're very lucky . . . so now you need to go home and tell your family you are thankful for them.
Rob:	*(A little uncomfortable with that thought)* I'm sure my family knows how I feel about them.
Dorine:	Yeah, both of our families know how much we appreciate them.
Penelope:	But you gotta say it! They need to hear it!
	(Silence)
Cecil:	Sir, can I ask you a question?
Rob:	Okay.
Cecil:	Do you have a wife?
Rob:	Yes . . .
Cecil:	Do you have a little boy?
Rob:	Two.
Cecil:	Have you told your wife and boys how thankful you are for them today?
Rob:	No.
Penelope:	Lady, you must have a mommy and a daddy . . . did you tell them why you're thankful for them on this Thanksgiving Day?
Dorine:	No, I haven't. I guess being with them is not enough?
Cecil:	No . . . Someday you'll turn around and they'll be gone. You gotta to say it now.
Dorine:	I don't think I know how . . .

▶ *Characterization: Cecil & Penelope Moment*

Cecil and Penelope create their own things. All of their props should be handmade with items one would find on the streets or in a trash bin. Try thinking about it like this: *What would a child create?* That's what Cecil and Penelope's creations should look like.

SOUND:	**CECIL AND PENELOPE'S BACKGROUND**
Penelope:	Cecil and me will show you how . . .

(PENELOPE and CECIL turn to each other)

	My dearest Cecil. Have I told you how thankful I am for you lately? I am thankful for all of you . . . from the top of your shiny head to the bottom of your funny feet. The best part of my life is sharing it with you. You make me laugh and sing . . . and I thank God every day that He gave you to me. Thank you, my dear Cecil.
Cecil:	My dearest Penelope. Even if you weren't so beautiful, I would be thankful for you anyway. You are the only person that has really ever cared for me . . . and I thank you for that. You don't laugh and make fun of me. You help me get through life . . . I would be lost without you. So on this special Thanksgiving Day, please don't forget how much I am thankful for you.

(CECIL and PENELOPE embrace)

Rob:	*(Looking at DORINE)* I think we need to get back. *(Stands)* I don't know about you, but I've got a few people to thank.
Dorine:	*(Standing)* Yes . . . a lot of people to thank. And I'll start with you, Cecil and Penelope. Thank you for showing us how wonderful it is to say "thank you" face-to-face with the ones you love.
Cecil:	Remember, you gotta say it!
Penelope:	Please go home and say it!
Rob:	Good-bye.
SOUND:	**FINAL TRANSITION OUT OF SKETCH**

(ROB and DORINE begin to leave . . . and when they're almost gone, DORINE pauses, then stops ROB. She reaches into the bag that ROB is carrying and pulls out a whole pumpkin pie. She turns to CECIL and PENELOPE and gives them the pie. DORINE and ROB smile and exit)

Cecil:	Look, Penelope. A pumpkin pie . . .
Penelope:	Isn't it beautiful!

(The two sit on the bench, take out their Styrofoam meals, and put them in their laps)

Penelope:	Cecil? What if one day you turn around and something's happened to me, and I'm gone?
Cecil:	*(Taking a second)* I would be very sad. But I would be thankful . . . because I know you'd be up with God—living in a big, big house!
Penelope:	I'm thankful for you, Cecil.

▸ *Characterization: Cecil & Penelope Moment*

Cecil and Penelope can find spiritual significance in just about everything they touch. Allow these two characters to relate object lessons like it is the most profound moment of their lives. They are serious about sharing with others!

Cecil: I'm thankful for you, Penelope.

Together: Happy Thanksgiving.

               (They now give thanks over their Styrofoam containers of Thanksgiving dinner and their pumpkin pie.)

LIGHTS: **FADE TO BLACK**

               END

GLOSSARY OF TERMS

Acting Area. The area of the stage setting on which the actor performs (may include areas off the normal stage). Usually split into portions for ease of reference: Up Stage, Center Stage, Stage Right, Stage Left, Apron, Offstage, etc.

Ad-Lib. Unrehearsed lines spoken during a performance 1) in reaction to other lines or 2) to transition from a mistake or dropped lines.

Aisle. A passage through seating.

Apron. Section of the stage floor which projects toward or into the auditorium. In proscenium theaters, the part of the stage in front of the main stage.

Aside. Lines spoken by an actor directly to the audience, not meant to be "heard" by other characters onstage.

Audition. Process where the director or casting director of a production asks performers to show what they can do. Tests the actors' response to a piece of text not prepared beforehand.

Backstage. The part of the stage and theater which is out of the sight of the audience; the service areas of the theater.

Beat. Short amount of time for a character to react, think, or pause in dialogue; smallest division of action in a play.

Blackout. A total, sometimes sudden, extinguishing of the stage lights, often at the end of a scene or act.

Blocking. The art of moving actors on and off the stage. This helps familiarize actors with their entrance and exit points. Also, the process of roughing out the moves as one actor relates to another in crossing the stage, sitting, standing, and all other actions.

"Break a Leg." A superstitious and widely accepted alternative to "Good luck" (which is considered bad luck in the theater).

Breaking Character. When actors do or say something inconsistent with the character they are portraying.

Call (Call Time). Notification of when production team, actors, and crew are scheduled to begin a rehearsal or performance.

Cast. The performers onstage.

Casting. The process the director goes through in choosing actors to perform the characters in a play.

Center Stage (CS). The middle portion of the stage—has good sightlines to all seats in the auditorium.

"Cheat Out" or "Open Up." This is simply a request for the actor to face more toward the audience. Although it is natural for people to face each other in real life, onstage the actor needs to make sure the audience can see and hear him or her.

Choreographer. Member of the production team responsible for setting dances and movement sequences during the production.

Comic Relief. A comic scene (or line) included in an otherwise straight-faced play to provide a relief from tension for the audience.

Costumes. Clothes worn by the actors onstage.

Cover. To make up dialogue and or blocking due to a mistake or accident onstage without breaking character.

Cross. The movement of an actor across the stage in any direction.

Cue. A signal to begin movement or speaking. There are many different types of cues. One is where an actor's cue to move or speak is dictated by the line (sentence) or word spoken by another actor. Another cue is when movement or speech is determined by sound/music or change in lighting. Sometimes an actor's cue will be another actor's movement onstage—anything from an actor entering the stage to one actor slapping another.

Curtain Call. At the end of a performance, the acknowledgment of applause by actors—the bows.

Dialogue. Words spoken onstage; usually involves more than one actor/character.

Director. Person carrying the ultimate responsibility for interpretation of script through control of actors and supporting production team.

Downstage (DS). The part of the stage closest to the audience.

Drama. The academic subject area into which theater falls.

Dress Rehearsal ("the Dress"). The final rehearsal before the performance. The actors are in costume and all technical problems should have been sorted out.

Ensemble. An acting group. Typically describes a group of performers who work well together, with no one actor outshining the others.

Entrance. 1) Place on a set through which the actor may appear. 2) Point in the script at which an actor appears onstage.

Exit. 1) The process of leaving the stage. 2) Point in the script at which an actor leaves the stage.

Fade. A fade is an increase, diminishment, or change in lighting or sound level.

Follow on Cue. A cue that is executed automatically after the previous one.

Hand Prop. Any prop handled by an actor.

Hit Your Mark. When an actor stands in the correct position (usually with regard to lighting), he or she is said to have "hit the mark."

House Lights. The decorative fixtures that light the auditorium while the audience is entering or leaving; usually they are dimmed or switched off during the performance.

Improvisation. When an actor who is "in character" makes up action or dialogue without prior scripting; often used in rehearsal or to cover other mistakes.

Intention. A single, temporary desire or goal that arises in a character within a scene.

Lighting Director. The individual in charge of working with the lighting crew to create a lighting design and run the lights during a performance.

Mime. Form of performance with no spoken words. Plot, character, etc., are conveyed to the audience by movement and gesture.

Monologue. A speech made by a single actor, usually in long paragraph form.

Motivation. The desires or goals of a character that propel him or her into action; the driving force of an inciting event that starts a story's progression.

Musical Director. The person in charge of the musical content of a show.

Notes. Following a rehearsal (or an early performance in a run), the director will give notes to the cast and crew about where to make changes, improvements, cuts, etc.

Objective. A single, temporary desire or goal that arises in a character within a scene. (Also called Intention.)

Offstage. Backstage area outside the performance area.

Open. To turn toward or face the audience.

Overture. The music that begins a performance.

Pace. The speed at which the story and action in a play runs.

Pantomime. Simply acting without words. This involves the use of the entire body, including facial expressions.

Part. An actor's part is his or her lines and directions; the whole performance of an individual.

Plot. The fundamental thread that runs through a story, providing the reason for the actions of the characters.

Preset. Used to describe any article or prop placed in its working area before the performance.

Principals (Primaries). The actors with lead or speaking roles in a show.

Projection. A request by a director for greater audibility from an actor. Not merely a matter of speaking louder, however; projection means to control volume, clarity, and distinctness so that the audience can better understand the lines being spoken.

Prompt. To feed an actor his next line when he has forgotten it. (Very unprofessional and a bad idea . . . but some people still do it!)

Pronunciation. Speaking clearly and precisely in order to be understood. It is important that the words being spoken can be heard clearly by everyone in the audience.

Props (short for "property"). Furnishings, set dressings, and all items large and small which cannot be classified as scenery, electronics, or wardrobe. Props handled by actors are called hand props, while props kept in an actor's costume are personal props.

Reader's Theater. Where the cast reads the play aloud with the script in hand, with or without gestures.

Rehearsal. The learning of the show by the cast and crew before a public performance.

Resolution. The point during a drama when the plotline reaches a conclusion and conflict is resolved.

Run-Through. A rehearsal at which all the elements of the production are put together in their correct sequence.

Scene. 1) A stage setting. **2)** The blocks or parts into which a play is divided. **3)** A particular setting of stage lighting that can be reproduced on demand.

Script. The text of the show, also containing information about settings, characters, costumes, etc., to aid the cast and crew.

Segue. Originally a musical term for an immediate follow-on; now used more generally for any immediate follow-on.

Set. All the scenery, furniture, and props used to create a particular scene.

Set Dressing. Props used to create atmosphere rather than having a function.

Sightlines. Lines indicating the limits of what an audience can see. The sightlines can be drawn on a plan or determined by someone in the auditorium.

Slapstick. Slightly manic but physical comedy that relies on often violent behavior to elicit laughter.

Stage Crew. Group of individuals who work behind the scenes setting props and scenery and handling the mechanical aspects of the production.

Stage Direction. In the script of a play, any instruction for the actors, or setting or character description.

Stage Left (SL). The left side of the stage as viewed by the cast facing the audience. Also Prompt Side, Camera Right.

Stage Right (SR). The right side of the stage as viewed by the cast facing the audience. Also Opposite Prompt, Camera Left.

Stage Set. All of the scenery in a scene. The stage set creates the physical setting—or sense of place—in which the action of a scene occurs.

Strike. To clear the stage of scenery and other materials, or to remove a specific article.

Supporting Cast. Actors who are not playing major parts.

Technical. The functions essential to a play other than those of the cast's actual interpretation of the script, particularly the set, lighting, etc.

Theme. The central idea of a play.

Typecast. When an actor or actress is cast repeatedly in the same kind of role or character. Happens with actors who have a distinctive look, voice, or stature.

Understudy. An actor who learns the part of another and is ready to step into their shoes, should they not be able to perform due to illness or some other reason.

Upstage. The part of the stage farthest from the audience.

Upstaging. Deliberately drawing focus onstage.

Walk-Through. Rehearsals at which the actors go through entrances, moves, and exits to make clear any changes or alterations that may be necessary.

Wardrobe. General name for the costume department, its staff, and the space they occupy.